Misa, Mesa, y Musa

VOLUME 2

LITURGY IN THE U.S. HISPANIC CHURCH

COMPILED AND EDITED BY

KENNETH G. DAVIS, o.f.m., Conv.

World Library Publications
the music and liturgy division of J.S. Paluch, Inc.
3708 River Road, Suite 400
Franklin Park, IL 60131-2158

ACKNOWLEDGEMENTS

The most enjoyable part of any publication is giving thanks to those who made it possible. In addition to our collaborators, I wish to thank Gonzalo Saldana of the Instituto Nacional Hispano de Liturgia and Eduardo Rivera of World Library Publications. I am grateful as well to Joel Schorn for his help with copyediting, and Catesby C. Clay, Jr., who assisted with the bibliography. The vocabulary was much aided through the kind offices of Sister Caridad Inda, the Reverend Raúl Gómez, and Father Manuel Sanahuja.

Several of our chapters are republished from fine journals. Hence, we acknowledge ¡Gracias! Magazine (Liturgy Training Publications of the Archdiocese of Chicago); Liturgical Minstry, New Theology Review, and Worship (Liturgical Press); Ministry & Liturgy (Resource Publications); and Liguorian Magazine (Liguori Publications).

Finally, my sincerest thanks as well to Sister Doris Turek, multicultural specialist of the Secretariat for the Liturgy of the United States Conference of Catholic Bishops.

—Kenneth G. Davis, O.F.M., Conv.

Published by World Library Publications. Compilation copyright © 2008, World Library Publications, the music and liturgy division of J. S. Paluch Company, Inc., 3708 N. River Road, Suite 400, Franklin Park, IL 60131-2158, 800-566-6150, www.wlpmusic.com

Cover image and interior page decoration: Supper at Emmaus copyright © G. E. Mullan. Used by permission.

Excerpts from: The Constitution on the Sacred Liturgy © Costello Publishing Co.; General Norms for the Liturgical Year and Calendar and General Instruction of the Roman Missal © International Commission on English in the Liturgy; Catechism of the Catholic Church, Built of Living Stones, "The Sign of Peace", and The Hispanic Presence © United States Conference of Catholic Bishops; Directory on Popular Piety and the Liturgy, Novo Millenio Ineunte, Decree on the Apostolate of the Laity, and "The Road to Cologne" © Libreria Editrice Vaticana; Perspectivas: Occasional Papers (Martell-Otero) © L.I. Martell-Otero; Hispanic Catholic Culture in the U.S. (Pérez) and The Treasure of Guadalupe (Matovina and Elizondo) © University of Notre Dame Press; The New Dictionary of Sacramental Worship (Fink and Larson-Miller), Worship (Woofenden), and The Mass (Jungmann) © Liturgical Press; How to Understand the Liturgy (Lebon) © Crossroad; St. Justin Martyr: The First and Second Apologies (Barnard) © L. M. Barnard, Paulist Press, Inc.; Caminemos con Jesús (Goizueta) © Orbis Books; Pastoral Music (Vela) © National Association of Pastoral Musicians; America (Matovina and Reese) © America Press Inc.; Cyril of Jerusalem (Yarnold) © Routledge. Pescador de Hombres © 1979, Cesareo Gabarain, and Desterrados © Juan Espinosa, published by OCP Publications, 5536 NE Hassalo, Portland, OR 97123. All rights reserved. Used with permission.

Every attempt has been made to contact copyright owners of quoted material. If any omission or infringement of copyright has occurred through oversight, upon notification amendment will be made in future editions.

This book was edited by Kenneth G. Davis, O.F.M., Conv. WLP editorial assistance provided by Mary Beth Kunde-Anderson and Marcia T. Lucey. Deb Johnston was the production manager. Design and layout by Chris Broquet. The book was set in Berkley, Bernhard Condensed and Eurostile. Printed in the United States of America.

WLP 012702   ISBN 978-1-58459-376-8

CONTENTS

PREFACE

Joyce Ann Zimmerman, C.PP.S.

When I was a very small child, we lived near my grandfather and several aunts and uncles. My earliest memory of Sundays is spending the time after Mass happily playing with my cousins while the adults visited. During the warm summer months my grandfather would sit on the porch in his favorite rocker, and I remember often climbing up on his lap to listen to him tell his favorite stories of living on the farm. I knew the names of his work horses by heart (the only name I can remember now is "Bessie"!). Then we moved away from these relatives, and I remember how Sundays were never quite the same. I not only missed seeing all my relatives, but I also missed the connection with extended family and shared traditions which taught me my own cultural heritage.

My first response to the invitation to write the preface to this book exploring diverse Hispanic liturgical and devotional expressions was, "Heavens, no!" I felt a Spanish-speaking person ought to write it. Then I said "yes" because I can at least claim two connections with Spanish-speaking people in the United States: I, too, come from an immigrant background which stresses strong family ties, and I, too, learned through my elders a deep love for Catholic faith and liturgical tradition.

Previously, the United States has proverbially been called a "melting pot." When immigrants began to arrive here from Europe, they tended to settle near each other in order to keep language, traditions, and cultural heritage alive. We took that for granted. This tendency was no less true for members of the Catholic faith; Catholics would be inclined to settle together in neighborhoods around their neighborhood church. Not too many decades ago, parishes were still relatively small and it would not be unusual to have a German American, Italian American, Portuguese American, and Hungarian American parish all within a few blocks of each other. The priests grew up speaking the language of the parish, understood and were imbued with its culture, and sometimes even were sons of the parish.

The immigration phenomenon of years ago still continues today with a new wave of immigrants, most of them non-western Europeans. Happily many of these new immigrants bring with them

Joyce Ann Zimmerman, C.PP.S.

their Catholic faith and heritage. Now we find Korean and Vietnamese parishes, sometimes with their own native-speaking priests or priests and pastoral ministers who have managed to learn at least the fundamentals of the language. Recent demographic statistics have shown us that the largest minority group in the U.S. is now Spanish-speaking, comprising about one quarter of the population.

Unlike many other immigrant groups, however, the Spanish-speaking population comes from many countries, making them very diverse. They share a common language and many cultural traditions as well as the Catholic faith and have stamped this faith with their own unique expressions: identity with the suffering Jesus, a great devotion to Mary, and sensitivity to the communion of saints through their appreciation of the extended family, to name some.

Just as I felt displaced when we moved away from relatives, and hunger for the familiarity of my cultural heritage shared with extended family as a child, so do these new immigrants experience a similar loss and longing. It is only just and proper that the Catholic Church responds positively to the challenge of ministering to these diverse members of the Body of Christ as the church did in the past. Where the population is sufficient, we might have whole parishes of Spanish-speaking people, with all the Masses and other services conducted in Spanish. In most cases, though, parishes are a "integrated," with a Spanish Mass taking its place alongside English ones and perhaps Masses in other languages. As the contributors to this volume clearly recognize, however, it is not sufficient simply to have Mass in Spanish, sing Spanish hymns, and accommodate at least some cultural traditions and customs. Liturgical inculturation cannot be achieved by mere "add ons," but only by truly respecting and expressing within the very structure of the rite the cultural genius of the community.

Liturgical inculturation is a challenging proposition at best! As I read the prepublication manuscript of this book, a great number of issues arose which brought me up short and led me to spend some time in reflection. Surely as readers study and pray the chapters of this book contributed by people experienced in facilitating liturgy and prayer for Spanish-speaking people and who deeply love this people and their culture, points for consideration will come to the fore for them, too. I offer here six points of my reflection.

First, at this particular historical period in the church, we are all struggling with liturgical renewal and inculturation (perhaps we have always struggled with them); we not only struggle to celebrate Mass for particular language groups, but for youth, children, charismatics, and others. We have a natural sense that the ritual structure must be adapted to suit the assembly who celebrates. A single rite was not always the norm for the western church, and liturgy has always undergone adaptations. In the latter part of the first millennium Charlemagne introduced the Latin rite beyond Rome to the various regions of his expanding empire in a brilliant tactic promoting unity in the empire. Nonetheless, there was strong resistance in some regions to celebrating with this unfamiliar rite (and some adaptations exist in Europe even today).

While it is indisputable that the Roman rite with its noble simplicity has been the western liturgical norm for over a thousand years, it remains, nonetheless, a rite derived from a particular cultural milieu. We might suggest that the liturgical renewal of the Second Vatican Council really addressed the inculturation issue: How can the Roman rite be better suited to peoples today, facing the challenges of the twenty-first century? How can it be adapted so that it is better suited to various cultures today? In a sense, then, we must all be engaged in a project of inculturation. And this task is not easy.

Second, inculturation is challenging enough in fairly homogeneous cultural groups such as we experienced in our recent past. But today we have no absolute commonality in either Spanish-speaking communities themselves or in our larger parishes of many cultural heritages, a situation which adds a further complication and challenge for real inculturation. This diversity, on the other hand, has a great benefit: We all bring insights, talents, and values to our prayer and liturgy, and the variations and differences serve to reveal both more aspects of the depth of the faith we share and also more authentic ways to inculturate liturgy.

Third, Jesus' "Do this in memory of me" was more than an invitation to take, bless, break, and give the gifts of bread and wine as the Body and Blood of Christ. It was also an invitation to conform our very lives to the dying and rising mystery of Jesus' saving event. First and foremost, this is what we do in liturgy: enact the Paschal Mystery ritually here and now in such a way that we are transformed more perfectly into being members of the Body of Christ, continuing Jesus' saving mission through our daily living in our world today. All inculturation must serve this fundamental purpose of liturgy. Any

Joyce Ann Zimmerman, C.PP.S.

inculturation elements introduced into the rite which undermine this fundamental purpose do not promote authentic inculturation.

Fourth, the *Constitution on the Sacred Liturgy* makes clear (no. 13) that there is an important distinction between liturgical prayer (which ritually enacts the Paschal Mystery) and devotional prayer (which is a splendid shaping of our personal prayer in order to effectively encounter Christ); in addition, the liturgy far surpasses devotional prayer and must be respected as such. It is helpful to make a distinction, then, between devotional prayers (Stations of the Cross, dramatizations of events in the life of Christ, and others) which the church does not so assiduously regulate, and liturgy itself which the church carefully regulates in order to ensure that the church celebrates universally one Eucharist. The very nature of the prayer always inculturates devotional prayer. Spanish-speaking peoples can teach all of us a great deal about having a healthy prayer life beyond gathering for liturgy. They can teach us much about the domestic church and the role of elders in handing on our faith tradition.

Fifth, as I mentioned earlier, legitimate inculturation of liturgy is never an "add on" but is always an integral part of the liturgy itself, seamlessly incorporated, which facilitates the assembly's grasp of the Paschal Mystery. For this reason, some of the more important and more often celebrated rituals proper to most Spanish-speaking Catholic communities are being published as "official" rituals (a good example in the U.S. is the *Quinceañera* celebration incorporated into the Mass), not as a way to control the rituals but as a way to ensure that these celebrations are brought in line with the purpose of liturgy. Other popular expressions of faith (*Las Posadas*, for example) may even take place at church (although more often in the neighborhood or home), but are not incorporated into liturgy as such because they arise out of devotional prayer and nourish popular piety.

Sixth, and finally, inculturation is not simply an unreflective accommodation of cultural expressions of faith into the liturgy. In addition to enacting the Paschal Mystery, liturgy always has as its purpose to challenge worshipers beyond their present experience in order to encounter Christ and each other in ever new ways. Liturgy always challenges us to change and moves us beyond where we are. And perhaps this is another reason why genuine inculturation of the liturgy is so difficult: Liturgy must always personally and communally challenge but never alienate, evoke but never stifle, be an expression of the experience of an immanent God who cares for and loves people at the same time liturgy takes people to an encounter with mystery and the transcendence of God.

This book is a pleasant balance of theology and practice, historical insight and contemporary challenge, examples of saints of the Americas and suggestions for adapting essential elements of the Eucharistic liturgy. To be sure, it is not the last word on inculturation of liturgy for Spanish-speaking people in the United States, nor is it meant to be. And not having the last word is a good thing—it reminds us that inculturation is such a critical area of study and practice that we ought never be finished with it; we can always learn and implement more, we can ever find fresh ways to encounter our God in all the majesty of mystery, compassion, and love.

In the last analysis, the final word on inculturation will be said only when we stand before God in beatific vision and glory, when we no longer need the symbols and stuff of this world to mediate the divine. Only then, enjoying everlasting life, will we experience fully the crowning goal of liturgical inculturation and, indeed, of all liturgy itself—eternal unity with our triune God: Father, Son, and Holy Spirit. To this God be all glory and praise, now and always.

Joyce Ann Zimmerman, C.PP.S.

INTRODUCTION:
LITURGY IS CHILD'S PLAY
Kenneth G. Davis

Readers of the original *Misa, Mesa y Musa* know that the title refers to the three elements of fiesta, namely Mass (*misa*), table/food (*mesa*), and cultural celebrations such as music, dance, and poetry (*musa*). As we celebrate the fiesta of the tenth anniversary of the original volume, I am in my twentieth year of ordination.

As a priest, I have been on the "inside" of the Mass at many a fiesta, but always on the "outside" of the *mesa* and *musa*. By that I mean that I presided and preached the Mass, often helped plan the readings and music as well, but only observed the rest of the fiesta rather than being directly involved in preparing the meal or cultural events.

All that changed when my goddaughter recently made her First Holy Communion. Because I was her godfather (*padrino* in Spanish), for the first time I was expected to take an active role in the entire fiesta. And I felt as unprepared as FEMA before Katrina!

But I dutifully arrived several days before the fiesta, and along with her parents and uncles and aunts, we got started. Gratefully, they had all been on the "inside" of fiestas before, but I was amazed and exhausted by everything that went into properly preparing all the other fiesta activities outside of Mass.

First, all the invitations were handmade as well as hand-delivered. Then all the *recuerdos* or little mementos given to each guest were also handmade, as was each centerpiece. Actually, everything was homemade in the sense that the entire fiesta was planned, prepared, and celebrated in my goddaughter's home.

The women began cooking days ahead of time in the small steaming kitchen while we men struggled with renting and hauling a huge tent, some twenty tables, and about two hundred chairs. Groceries and beverages had to be purchased as well as transported, and it seemed that after every trip to the store someone remembered something else that was needed. Of course after all this the home had to be cleaned and the lawn manicured. Lights and decorations were created and strung.

I finally got a break from the heavy lifting when my goddaughter, her godmother, and I went to outfit her as the custom for costume requires. I hate shopping even more than hauling tables and chairs, but I was determined to be a good godfather. So we bought her a white dress with lace fringes, matching shoes, socks, and gloves, as well as a crown for her head made of baby's breath. She and her godmother cooed and clucked over every item, and by the time they were done I was glad to be back to the sweating, driving, worrying, and struggling to get everything rushed but ready in time.

Maybe I sweated and struggled more because it was all so new to me. I didn't even know how much work a piñata was, but believe me, after it was full of candy it was heavy—and we had two! My middle-aged body felt even older when, while stuffing candies into the piñatas with my goddaughter, I mused, "One day I will be doing this with your daughter," to which she responded rather clinically, "Oh no, *Padrino*, by then you'll be all old and dead."

Finally, and thankfully, everything was ready. By ten in the morning the church was full of beaming parents and relatives, friends, and classmates. And with her dress and crown my goddaughter did look like the "precious princess" I always called her. After Mass we walked the few blocks to her house to begin the rest of the fiesta.

Like the little princess, everything was ready. The lighted house shone, the handmade decorations glistened, the two piñatas were hoisted. Tables and chairs were lined up like a military procession with unwrinkled table clothes framing perfect centerpieces. At each place waited the personal *recuerdo*, and permeating all was the smell of fajitas and frijoles. That was about 11:00 a.m.

By six that evening the house looked like a Baghdad no-go zone. The lawn was scattered with candy wrappers and remnants of piñatas. The *recuerdos* and centerpieces were stripped, the tables out of alignment, a couple of chairs toppled. Litter covered stained tablecloths, and some of the lights were dangling. Ants had begun an invasion of a water cooler; the only bathroom smelled like wet diapers.

And the precious princess? Her crown was gone, her face was smeared, the lace on her dress was frayed, and one shoe flapped loose as she ran by with the other kids in a gaggle of giggle—she was ecstatic! When she saw my exhausted face, she rushed to me with sticky hands outstretched and said, "*Padrino*, do you need a hug?"

_____ *Kenneth G. Davis, OFM Conv.*

Padrino needed a double tequila! But I settled for the joy that suffused her face like sunlight on surf, and thought: Liturgy is child's play.

We had spent days and nights, as well as considerable stress and money, on making the fiesta perfect. And in less than six hours she and her friends had blasted it all into litter and laughter. But, of course, that is the point.

Liturgy, like fiesta, is ancient, but it is not a museum. We don't work so hard to create the art and environment or music (*musa*), the table of Word and Eucharist (*mesa*) for a Mass (*misa*) so that only the perfectly behaved or properly educated can be shepherded through without touching or messing anything. The whole point is that we sacrifice in liturgical ministry to create order so that the assembly can gather under the power of the Spirit who comes blasting through to throw us all into the holy chaos of conversion. That's what both fiesta and liturgy are for. Both create a place so orderly it is safe enough for even children to be childlike. To enjoy fiesta they have to destroy it, just as to be Eucharist we must consume it.

After my first total immersion in a whole fiesta, I was exhausted but not unhappy because the precious princess and all her little guests were rapturous; they knew they were loved just as they were: boisterous and destructive, loud and hungry, dirty and wild. Liturgy, like fiesta, is the serious work of creating a frame, not to domesticate the Spirit, but to make us safe enough to undergo its untamable Presence. Real Presence or the presence of the Real is like the essence of a child's happy squeal: It is adorable only when endurable.

So why is liturgy child's play? Well, we are (and should be) very adult in our disciplined preparation for liturgy. We order ourselves so that there is a designated time and place properly arranged as well as ministers carefully chosen and trained. And once we have done the adult thing and settled into our sacred space at the appointed time with everything ready, the childlike Holy Spirit enters and very likely blasts through all our carefully controlled preparations. Like a child at a fiesta, the Holy Spirit is not invited into our liturgy simply to observe with proper reserve. The very orderliness of our liturgy exists to give the Spirit a chance to upset the very ordinariness of our lives. Liturgy is not coercive, but it is subversive when it opens the doors of our gated community to the incursion of conversion.

So this book is about how liturgy is a kind of indult from being only adult. Perhaps the seditious Spirit says, "Invite in all the people the census forgot"—the point of Part I, "Hospitality." Part II, "Liturgy and Devotions," introduces the insurgency of good friends of the Holy Spirit that she might want readers to know. Or she may smilingly remind us that it was once just as revolutionary to celebrate Saint Patrick in Lent as it now appears to honor Our Lady of Guadalupe as an icon of Advent as suggested by Part III, "The Liturgical Year." And, of course, no one knows radical rhythm like the Spirit as clearly expressed in Part IV, "Music." The Spirit inspires innovative proclamation by example and symbol as well as word, all discussed in Part V, "Preaching." And finally, while reading Part VI, the Spirit might prod us grumpy grown-ups: "You know those young people you find rebellious? Well, they're my friends, too. And those migrants remind me that the Holy Family didn't have visas either. Worship with them; they can teach you a lot about me."

The Spirit is inclusive, and so is our list of contributors. They represent both genders, lay and ordained, and seven distinct countries. Together they have produced this book, which we hope our readers will relish like a fiesta. We put in the hard work, and now throw it all open to the childlike Holy Spirit who breathes in the breast of each of you, our readers.

Recall, however, that the Spirit speaks to us personally, but not privately. The Spirit is inclusive, not exclusive. And that is why *Misa, Mesa, y Musa Volume 2* is published. Without attention to all God's people, especially the very youthful Hispanics, our liturgies—like too many an empty church—feel like a museum. Without openness, ancient rituals atrophy. Authentic worship can never contain the spendthrift Spirit any more than budgets constrain grandparents at Christmas. And good grandparents welcome *all* their grandchildren, especially those most in need, with hospitality, respect for their heroes and heroines, appropriate music (even dance and gesture), words of wisdom, and fondness for all the year's feasts of birthdays and anniversaries. The parts of this book cover each of those themes just like a fiesta at a grandparent's home. Because good ministers, like good grandparents, understand that liturgy is child's play, not only law. While it requires discipline, it also always requires wonder and awe.

—Kenneth G. Davis, ofm Conv.

PART I
Hospitality

MESTIZO LITURGY:
A *MESTIZAJE* OF THE ROMAN AND
HISPANIC RITES OF WORSHIP
Arturo Pérez Rodriguez

Setting the scene

St. Francis of Assisi Parish is known as the "mother church" for Chicago's Spanish-speaking community. For nearly one hundred years Hispanics have found San Francisco, as it is commonly known, to be a place of refuge. New arrivals to Chicago know that Spanish is the first language of this parish. It is also a church that practices the traditions of popular religion as an ordinary part of life. This mother church embraces ethnic and national Hispanic diversity through its religious devotions and images. *Guadalupe* as the Patroness of the Americas stands with *Nuestra Señora de la Caridad* (Our Lady of Charity, Patroness of Cuba) and *Nuestra Señora de la Providencia* (Our Lady of Providence, Patroness of Puerto Rico) as well as with *San Martín de Porres* and *Santa Teresa de Ávila*, among others. In the recent past St. Francis became an example of the Paschal Mystery at work within the Hispanic community. The events of the past three years echo within the collective consciousness of Hispanic people throughout the nation where parishes have closed.

A number of years ago archdiocesan regional planning sessions resulted in the decision to close San Francisco. It was to merge with another parish four blocks away. This death experience, like other parish closings, was painful and beyond people's comprehension. On a cold February evening in 1996, on the eve of the scheduled date for San Francisco's demolition, a group of parishioners moved into the gutted church building. Though too complex to describe for our purposes here, their action resulted in restudy, reevaluation, and eventual reopening of the parish.

St. Francis serves more than two thousand people every weekend. An experience of death has become an experience of resurrection. As the resurrected Christ appeared to his disciples with wounds in his side, hands, and feet, giving them a new mission, in a similar way this local community, as the wounded body of Christ, is struggling to discern its new resurrected mission. Each worship experience is a challenge to incarnate the Paschal Mystery of these past three years through the practices of the official liturgy of the Roman Catholic Church as well as with the expressions of Hispanic popular religion. Our challenge is to remain faithful to both while living anew the death and resurrection of this local community of faith.

We begin with this panoramic view of San Francisco in order to set the scene, to situate specifically and concretely the reality of the Hispanic community. Within each Hispanic community there is a history of rejection and integration, of struggle and success, of death and new life. This history is part and parcel of the reality that we Hispanic people face. The closing and reopening of St. Francis is just another example. The Paschal Mystery as Hispanic communities celebrate it is not only a liturgical experience but also an experience of the wounded resurrected Lord in our midst. This rejection and integration is certainly not unique to the Spanish-speaking community of the United States. It is part of the history of many immigrant groups. Yet each group faces it in different ways. Vietnamese, Hmong, Korean, and other Asian peoples are the newest participants in this dying and rising process. The Paschal Mystery will translate into their lives in a new way.

I direct the following to non-Hispanic liturgical pastoral agents who build bridges, linking the Roman rite with the Hispanic pattern of prayer. These words are also directed to Hispanic persons who desire to reflect upon their own particular religious cultural genius so as to affirm and appreciate more fully this well of life from which we drink of the presence of God. It is presumed that we, non-Hispanic and Hispanic liturgical ministers, will first direct our attention to the specific community we are called to serve. We must set the scene for our ministry. We situate ourselves in the specific cultural, ethnic, historical, liturgical, and prayer traditions of our individual communities. It is here that we come face to face with the tensions, temptations, and experiences of a *mestizaje* experience of the Roman and Hispanic rites of worship.

We first look at *mestizaje* as a liturgical experience of the Paschal Mystery. Second, we identify three foundational approaches within this experience and the tensions and temptations they contain. Next I offer two examples of a mestizo liturgy. They give testimony to what those who are open to the Spirit of these moments can achieve. We conclude with a suggestion for a Sunday mestizo liturgy.

Mestizo liturgy: The goal

Simply stated, *mestizaje* is the blending and mixing of different realities. Hispanic *mestizaje* is a rich, diverse experience of life. In the *mestizaje* context one finds the historical antecedents of the sixteenth century, when the Spanish and indigenous worlds came together in a violent religious and cultural clash. This clash resulted in the birth of a new mestizo people. It was the first of two conquests. The second occurred when the United States government annexed parts of Mexico and therefore its citizens into a "new world." The clash between different religious and cultural worldviews persisted. The present day continues to echo these experiences as both ecclesial and national institutions wonder about how to integrate the Hispanic world into their own. Though many doors have opened, a great deal of work still remains in truly welcoming the Hispanic community with the gifts of its culture and religious expression.

The Hispanic community has learned how to blend, to adjust to a given situation without losing its identity, specifically through maintaining the practices of popular religion. These practices adjust to the economic, geographic, climatic, urban, or rural situations in which they are practiced. These celebrations not only maintain but also nourish a Hispanic worldview. For this reason they are so valuable and resilient. The Hispanic way of prayer clashes at times with the normative way of prayer in the Roman rite when the latter is identified also with the majority white community.

With some qualification, we can say that the Hispanic people confront a "one way attitude" of life. This one way usually means a white majority way. Liturgy reflects life and therefore becomes a prime venue for these two attitudes to meet face to face. The Hispanic asks the question "Why?" "Why do things have to be done in this way?" "Why are these feasts celebrated in this pattern?" Some people often misinterpret these questions to mean "my way or your way." They seem them as either/or, win/lose moments. The *mestizaje* approach is neither my way nor your way but a third, fourth, or fifth way that yields to "our way." *Mestizaje* is a creative blending of different approaches that includes parts of all to form a new way.

St. Francis offers an example of this blending. Before preparing final drawings for the church's reconstruction, open parish meetings were held highlighting the liturgical needs of the Roman rite. These sessions revealed the emotional intensity of the people's need to

Arturo Pérez Rodriguez

preserve the traditions of this local community through a restoration of all shrines, areas for candles, and murals. Tension was high. If the church building was to serve this community, it would have to blend the Roman rite with the Hispanic. It is important to look at both.

The Roman rite offers a specific pattern of prayer for public worship. Yet these rites by their very nature, as the *Constitution on the Sacred Liturgy* states, "should radiate a noble simplicity; they should be short, clear, and unencumbered by useless repetitions; they should be within the people's powers of comprehension, and not as a rule require much explanation" (no. 34). One can define in a cultural way what "simple, short, clear, and within the people's powers of comprehension" means. We need to remember that this statement is itself a cultural expression of a Roman, European experience of worship that highlights, values, and sees clean, organized, and unencumbered liturgy as the norm. This statement is neither negative nor positive but simply *one* approach. The wisdom of this Roman pattern of prayer is that it also contains an attitude that people often forget or downplay: its openness to incorporating other cultural approaches. We owe a debt of gratitude to Anscar Chupungco, who in his various writings on inculturation has continued to remind us that the noble simplicity of the Roman rite made it easier for it to be incarnated in the faith experiences of each people it encountered. In our terms we could say that the Roman rite was meant from the beginning to become a *mestizaje* experience of worship.

The other ingredient in this *mestizaje* is the Hispanic pattern and expression of prayer. Though not found in any ritual book, the practices of popular religion define a Hispanic rite. These practices are ways the Hispanic community identifies its needs, names its own experiences, and affirms its own relationship with God. The Latin American Bishops Conference clearly states in the magisterial documents of Puebla: "By the religion of the people, popular religiosity, or popular piety (*Evangelii nuntiandii*, 48), we mean the whole complex underlying beliefs rooted in God, the basic attitudes that flow from these beliefs, and the expressions that manifest them. It is the form of cultural life that religion takes on among a given people. In its most characteristic cultural form, the religion of the Latin American people is an expression of the Catholic faith. It is a 'people's Catholicism' " (444). Though written for the Latin American reality, this statement resonates deeply within the Hispanic community of the United States.

This people's way of expressing faith becomes a people's liturgy.

The open liturgical attitude Puebla takes is evident when we read: "We must see to it that the liturgy and the common people's piety cross-fertilize each other, giving lucid and prudent direction to the impulses of prayer and charismatic vitality that are evident today in our countries. In addition, the religion of the people, with its symbolic and expressive richness, can provide the liturgy with creative dynamism. When examined with proper discernment, this dynamism can help to incarnate the universal prayer of the church in our culture in a greater and better way" (465). Cross-fertilization can be understood to be another expression for *mestizaje*: Two forms of prayer blend to become a new form of prayer. The creative dynamism inherent within the Roman and Hispanic rites forms a mestizo liturgy.

Mestizo liturgy moves us beyond *only* using Spanish, or *only* singing Spanish music, or *only* placing serapes on altars. In the light of *mestizaje* these things take on a minimalist attitude that the document *Environment and Art in Catholic Worship* describes (*EAW*, 14). Mestizo liturgy moves us beyond *only* waiting for big feasts in order to Hispanize the liturgy. Mestizo liturgy becomes a people's liturgy when the expressions of popular religion are regularly present in the celebration of the Sunday worship experience.

The people of San Francisco parish, like so many other Hispanic people, see the "old patterns of prayer" as though they were living realities, as though they were the community's grandparents. The parish reverences and honors these "old ones" for their wisdom and counsel, for what they teach about the mysteries of life, for how they help us speak with God. They are revelations of the mystery of Christ present in our grace and our sin, in our gifts and our limits, in our light and in our shadow. They help us to face the tensions and temptations of blending not only rites but also lives into a new experience of faith.

Foundational approaches: Tensions and temptations

After one Sunday Mass at San Francisco an elderly woman brought her eight-year-old granddaughter to me for a blessing. Her request was not for an ordinary blessing that people often ask for at the end of Mass. Nor was this a blessing for a child *espantado* ("shocked and frightened") by some dream or traumatic event. It was a blessing that would help this child "open her mouth" and speak clearly. It was

Arturo Pérez Rodriguez

evident that the young girl had a speech difficulty. The grandmother asked that I would touch the front-door key of the church to the child's mouth while praying for her healing. I confess that my own inherent pragmatic liturgical attitude immediately kicked in with questions about doctors, treatments, and therapies, all of which the family was using. Words about the sacrament of the sick hung unconnected in the air between us.

Hoping to sidestep the key issue I mentioned that the church had no front-door key because padlocks were still in use. Without a moment's hesitation the elderly woman said that the tabernacle key would do just fine. My own interior struggle knew that this was not "my way" of dealing with such realities, nor was it my way of blessing, yet it was her way. In the church proper I improvised a rite of anointing using the key as part of the introductory prayer. Interiorly I prayed that God would "open" this child's mouth while opening my mind and heart. Grandmother and granddaughter left after lighting a candle at the shrine of Jesus the *Nazareno*. Sitting alone in the church afterwards, I reflected on my own initial hesitation and final response. This experience again reminded me that spirituality, attitude, and images of God are foundational elements of a mestizo liturgy.

Spirituality

Mestizo liturgy is not easy. A foundational approach within mestizo liturgy involves spirituality. Most of us have been taught and formed in various schools of spirituality, be they the traditional ways of Teresa of Ávila, Francis of Assisi, Ignatius of Loyola, or the contemporary ways of creation or enneagram spiritual practices. The liturgical spirituality of the Roman rite has also formed us. We acknowledge that the renewal of the liturgy was not an end in itself. The renewal meant for us to reform our lives in the light of the Paschal Mystery we celebrate. This orientation is the liturgy's spirituality. Through our private expressions of prayer we integrate personal and communal aspects of spirituality into our liturgy. Full, active, and conscious participation in the liturgy translates into an experience that is fully human, that blends all aspects of life—emotional, mental, physical, intellectual, and spiritual—into one connected experience. Liturgy touches us in ways that are beyond our comprehension. In this sense the liturgy remains a mystery to us. It is a work of the Spirit. In mestizo liturgy a different form of spirituality expresses itself. It is a different, fully human experience of the mystery of God present among us.

Hispanic spirituality is a sensual experience that sees everything in creation as holding the possibility of an encounter with God. A simple key touching a child's mouth makes as much sense as anointing her forehead and hands with blessed oil. Both are instruments that school us in the way that God breaks open the moment to reveal graced Presence. From this perspective Hispanic spirituality offers the pastoral agent a different and often challenging way of seeing not only liturgy but also God at work within this event.

This way of seeing can be tension-filled because it is not our customary approach. A situation confronts us that is beyond not only our own individual experiences of prayer but also our known way of doing liturgy. We may be tempted to bypass the moment, say "no," or simply do what we are comfortable with. As liturgical pastoral agents we cannot be tourists in someone else's experience. We cannot be curious, superficial, or judgmental of their religious experience.

In order to get behind the people's experience, we are called to move into the tensions and temptations we face. We do this when we begin to practice Hispanic popular religion in our own moments of private prayer, thereby integrating them into our spirituality. We become familiar with a different way of making the sign of the cross, a mantra-like quality of praying a litany, a touch of the hand or foot of a statue in church, the promise of lighting a candle for our intention. We do this initially with a certain sense of unease until we remember that the Hispanic community is being asked to do the same thing through the Roman rite. As much as learning a new language is an experience in humility, so is learning a new language of prayer an openness to the Spirit. Mestizo liturgy is founded on mestizo spirituality. It is a blending of various schools of prayer.

Attitude

The second foundational approach in mestizo liturgy bases itself on our attitude. Attitude cannot be taught. It can only be learned through life. Mark Francis and I speak about this fact in our book, *Primero Dios: Hispanic Liturgical Resource*. Liturgical pastoral agents sometimes demonstrate a condescending, paternalizing attitude toward Hispanic people as though Hispanics have not yet been informed and educated in the "proper ways" of doing liturgy. The attitude can take an aggressive form when it simply rejects popular religion as superstitious, superfluous, and unnecessary. This attitude sees the expressions of popular religion to be in conflict with the norms of "good" liturgy.

On the other hand, in efforts to be sensitive to people's concerns, questions arise about the meaning of a particular tradition. Answers are not usually forthcoming because one can misinterpret the attitude behind the question as being judgmental, or because the people themselves do not know the origins and meanings of these practices. This situation may be an example of people being too close to the trees to see the forest. People see the expressions of popular religion simply as "the way we do this." The practice of the *presentación del niño* (the presentation of a child in the church) occurs in different areas of Mexico. In some regions it is completely unknown. This practice can take place forty days after birth, or when the child reaches his or her third birthday. What is important is the event celebrated rather than the words used. There are no precise words, just a prayer of blessing over the child, with his or her parents and *padrinos* (godparents). Popular religion places more emphasis on the action, the gesture, the symbol, rather than on the text or the words.

Undoubtedly this practice can produce a tense and frustrating situation for both people and minister alike. We, as liturgical agents, may be tempted to retreat by simply "doing whatever the people want," thereby not seeing the evangelical opportunity a given moment and practice contain. By the careful questioning and acceptance of popular traditions, the "seeds of the gospel" they contain can be nourished to yield a surprising spiritual harvest for both people and minister alike. Good catechetical preparation draws out the gospel meaning and enhances the practice. The *presentación del niño* can be united with the understanding and use of the oil of catechumens if it occurs before baptism. It is an enrichment of the Roman and Hispanic rites. Understandably this means walking a tightrope not only in terms of what we have come to know as "good" liturgy but also in seeing popular religion as part of the living word of God in mestizo liturgy.

Images of God

The images of God each of us uses are not the same. Though one could provide many examples, we offer two here: Jesus and Mary. The Roman liturgy reveals the Paschal Mystery through the image of the resurrected Lord. Through this triumph over death the promise of new life is fulfilled. We share in this resurrection experience through our liturgy. This image of God in the person of Jesus does not translate into the Hispanic community in the same way.

We can see the reopening of San Francisco parish as God's listening to the people's novenas and *mandas* (promises of prayer or sacrifice). We can see the focus of these prayers and *mandas* in the popularity (witnessed by the number of candles) of the life-size statue of Jesus *el Nazareno*, depicting the beaten, bloody, flagellated Christ. It is a vividly grotesque, realistic image of what scourging can do to human flesh. The Hispanic community's image of Christ interprets this moment in Christ's life as one of vulnerability like their own. It is an image of God who does not identify with us from "the outside looking in" but rather from the "inside looking out" of the Hispanic experience. It is an image of God who knows what rejection and brutality mean. In the writings of Hispanic theologians, the passion and crucifixion of Christ witness to the saving event of our life, but also to the fact that here in this death experience the Hispanic community already finds resurrection. It is in suffering that life is given. The image of Christ's sufferings mirrors the community's sufferings. Here in this gruesome moment the community shares and already celebrates hope. In this passion, life continues in a new way.

The tension that lies within this imagery is evident. Some people would see the *Nazareno* as contradicting the image the liturgy proposes. The Resurrection is our heart's desire and the promise in which we live and die. We may be tempted to eliminate these bloody images from church. We may look for ways to avoid highlighting them in our liturgies. We may hope to replace them with gentler, kinder depictions of Christ.

The resurrected Christ presents an image of God that is too clean, too orderly, too successful. The experiences of life teach us that life is messy, painful, mysterious, and beyond our control. There are no easy answers to all of life's hurts. The *Nazareno* is not in conflict with the resurrected Christ. It does not present a fatalistic approach to God. It embraces gruesome events by making us face them in a vividly human way. The image asks us to see through the brutality and find hope that only belief in life after death, as we see in the wounded resurrected Christ, can give.

Our second example is Mary. The Roman rite struggles to find a place for her. Though she is venerated through proper feasts, new

_____ *Arturo Pérez Rodriguez*

prefaces, and renewed devotions, many still look upon her as a focus more for private prayer. New images of Mary depict her pregnancy and her home life in caring for the child Jesus and Joseph. Though important as model and example of the Christian life, she remains more an object for personal reflection than community prayer. In saying this I believe that the liturgy does "objectify" the person of Mary by her "second-class" standing. Though words about her importance in the mystery of salvation are plentiful, the person of Mary seems aloof, distant, unrelated. Perhaps this perception provides some of the reasons why present-day miraculous apparitions of the *Virgen* have become devotions for many people.

María, *la Virgen Madre de Dios*, takes on a personal relational quality for the Hispanic community through her multiple titles. She is known as *La Dolorosa* or *La Soledad, La Guadalupe, La Virgen de la Caridad*, and *La Purísima*, to give only a few names. Each Central and Latin American and Caribbean country has its own national titles for *La Virgen*. She is woven into the common experiences of life. She is more than a devotion. She becomes the feminine image of God.

Hispanic culture sees creation as coming from a God who is both masculine and feminine. This mestizo quality is not "either/or" but "both at the same time." The *mestizaje* perspective sees no contradiction here. It is obvious that if God is not also feminine, then God is incomplete. It is through this imagery that God is more approachable, more fully human, more easily integrated with the feminine qualities, attributes, and values that form a more perfect image of God.

The images of Mary according to the Roman rite and *La Virgen* according to the Hispanic rite are not in competition. Pastoral ministers feel the tension to simplify Marian devotion and imagery within the liturgy. The Hispanic community sees that the multiple images of *La Virgen* in church only enhance her availability. The essence of Marian devotion is that "*La Virgen María*" is a bridge to God through her humanity. She is our connection to the mystery of God at work in us. She is God's feminine, maternal touch in our humanity. Seeing the Presence of God within her life, her images, and her devotion strengthens our faith and our bonds to one another.

As we previously mentioned, mestizo liturgy is not easy. As we have seen, it is founded on a mestizo spirituality that incorporates the spiritual schools of the Roman liturgy and the religious practices of Hispanic popular religion. Practice does not necessarily make perfect, but practice of this form of spirituality connects Hispanic and non-Hispanic pastoral agents in touching the Presence of God. Our attitude defines "good liturgy." Opening our minds and hearts means listening to the "seeds of the gospel" inherent in popular religion. The gospel challenges the entire community to witness to the presence of God found in the diversity of creation. God is visible in images of faith, such as *El Nazareno* or *La Virgen María*. These are dynamic, active revelations of God. They do not comfortably fit into a preconceived notion of God. What remains for us is a look at two examples of mestizo liturgy.

Two examples of mestizo liturgy

The communities and liturgical pastoral ministers of Chicago's Epiphany Parish and San Antonio's San Fernando Cathedral would be the first to say they are only beginning. Yet each of the following examples is in a way a triumph in approaching a mestizo liturgical experience. These parishes have successfully blended the Roman and Hispanic rites into a mestizo liturgy proper for their communities. The criteria for making this statement do not come from a perfectly planned and celebrated liturgy. Rather, they come from the way that people in the community have encountered the Paschal Mystery in a personal way. This encounter has moved them, changed them, and encouraged them to witness to the presence of God in their daily lives.

The Day of the Dead

November 2 is the liturgical feast of All Souls and for many Mexican people the celebration of the popular religious practices of the Day of the Dead. On this day they build home altars commemorating family members who have died. They place pictures, candles, flowers, food, incense—anything that brings the memory of the deceased home—on this altar. In these ways they celebrate death annually as another part of life; the dead are gone from our sight but continue to live and have their place among us. On this day people live out their belief in life after death.

Chicago's Southwest Side is made up of bungalow homes and three-flat apartment buildings that house not only families but the tensions and conflicts of overcrowding, working double shifts, and struggling to make ends meet. It is also the home of different street gangs. Rivalries produce clashes that result in drive-by shootings.

Death is an active presence among the Hispanic families of this community.

Epiphany Parish resides in these surroundings. With the members of the parish liturgy team, the local non-Hispanic pastor reflected on their annual Day of the Dead feast in relationship to the reality of violence and death in their neighborhood. The parish youth included gang youth. After initial meetings and personal contacts, the parish extended an invitation to them to build an altar for the members of their gang who had died. The altar would stand among the others in the church. An evening candlelit procession formed the entrance rite of the Mass for the Day of the Dead. It blended not only religious liturgical traditions but also people from this parish in a different way.

Through this practice parishioners came to know these particular young men. The two groups established individual and personal confidences. Families were surprised to see these young people in church attending the evening Mass on November 2. The pastor and various members of the liturgy team became trusted individuals for these gang-related parishioners. Their relationship through counsel, jobs, and friendship continued beyond November's feast day. The Day of the Dead celebration became a day of connections for the parish.

Good Friday at the Cathedral of San Fernando

Good Friday is generally one of the pivotal days of the year for the Hispanic community. San Fernando Cathedral, located in the center of San Antonio, Texas, has developed a mestizo liturgy around this feast. The liturgy begins at 9:00 a.m. in the *mercado*, the local tourist market, located six blocks from the cathedral. There among a crowd of Good Friday tourists and parishioners the Passion is enacted, beginning with Pilate condemning Jesus to death and releasing Barabbas. Through the street named *La Via Dolorosa* Christ carries his cross. Children are attentive and curious to see what is happening. Men and women shed tears. Everyone follows the procession slowly to the steps of the cathedral for the crucifixion.

In the early afternoon the *Siete Palabras* (meditation on the Seven Last Words of Christ) is held in the church. The Communion service of the Good Friday liturgy follows it. The celebration of the Word has already taken place in the street in the morning. The early evening finds the church still crowded with people who have gathered for the *Pésame* (the Condolence Service for Mary) and the *Entierro* (the Burial of Jesus).

Close to 9:00 p.m. the day's liturgy ends with another street procession and the touching of a statue of the dead Jesus. Each person leaves a simple flower. These flowers become Jesus' tomb.

People are not touching a cold statue but coming into contact with the warm human reality of the death and resurrection of Jesus throughout the day. These events celebrate the Paschal Mystery in such a way that people did not understand it any more intellectually, but it is now more approachable. Like a living icon these religious events draw people into living the reality of the mystery of God's presence among them. Both the Roman and Hispanic rites blend into a new liturgical experience that brings home the power and mystery they contain. People of this local parish proclaim their faith to the entire city of San Antonio. Good Friday at San Fernando invites people to reflect upon their full, active, and conscious participation not only in their parish but also in their relationship to their city.

Conclusion: Sunday mestizo liturgy

Mestizo liturgy on a regular Sunday basis is the goal. Developing this regular pattern of prayer requires discipline—the acknowledgment of the personal limits of both community and pastoral agents—and discernment. The Hispanic community does not have all the answers and insights into mestizo liturgy. It is dependent upon the sensitive, open-minded, and open-hearted questioning by non-Hispanic liturgical pastoral agents who also bring their gifts and talents to the table of the Lord. Non-Hispanic ministers need the Hispanic community to stretch their imaginations and break stereotypes of the way that community prayer through the practices of popular religion reveals God. Discipline in developing structures and liturgical plans requires of both parties trust, confidence, and affection.

Discernment of the Spirit of God requires a sense of contemplation, of seeing the transparent presence of God in these moments. Mestizo liturgy expresses this discernment. A suggested pattern for a Sunday mestizo liturgy may look like this:

Gathering Rite

Entrance Hymn

Traditional Sign of the Cross: *Por la señal de la santa cruz de nuestros enemigos Señor, líbranos, Dios nuestro, en el nombre del Padre, del Hijo, y del Espíritu Santo. Amén.*

_____ *Arturo Pérez Rodriguez*

On any given Sunday a *Presentación* or Welcome is given: The *Presentación de Niños* and Anointing with the Oil of Catechumens is celebrated. Parents present their newborns and children to the community as an initiation into the process of baptism. The priest anoints them with oil and prays for their wellbeing.

Or: The parish youth who are preparing for a *Quince Años* (fifteenth birthday celebration) are welcomed. They receive special recognition in the assembly both in seating and in prayer.

The Opening Prayer follows.

Liturgy of the Word

After the homily, couples preparing for marriage present themselves to the community in a ceremony in which they ask for the community's blessing.

Liturgy of the Eucharist

The Eucharistic Prayer is dialogical and musical in the pattern of the Eucharistic Prayers for Children.

Dismissal Rite

Representatives of the parish's elderly and the priest bless parents with their children and couples preparing for marriage in the traditional manner.

Every Sunday would be different in terms of the various groups or feasts celebrated. Yet every Sunday would be the same in the sense of following a similar pattern of prayer. Discipline and discernment would be necessary to develop a mestizo liturgy appropriate for the local community of faith.

San Francisco Parish has been in the middle of rebuilding, restoring, and renovating the church and, more importantly, its liturgical life. The reconstruction of the traditional main altar and side altars as well as the creation of a new ambo, baptistery, and altar serve as concluding examples. The huge traditional altars are homes for the saints and the practices of devotion for this community. They are the connection with the past. They are important because they form the backdrop for the new ambo, altar, and baptistery, the design of which will mirror them.

These new pieces will bring into sharp focus the death and resurrection of this parish. The old and new cannot exist without the other. Both reflect the other. Together they symbolize a liturgy in which both Roman and Hispanic rites form a *mestizaje* of the Paschal Mystery.

References

Chupungco, Anscar J. *Liturgical Inculturation: Sacramentals, Religiosity, and Catechesis.* Collegeville, Minnesota: Pueblo, 1992.

————. *Beyond Inculturation.* Washington, DC: Pastoral Press, 1994.

Elizondo, Virgilio. *Galilean Journey.* Maryknoll, New York: Orbis Books, 1983.

————. *The Future Is Mestizo.* Bloomington, Indiana: Meyer Stone Books, 1988.

Environment and Art in Catholic Worship. Washington, DC: United States Conference of Catholic Bishops Committee on the Liturgy, 1978. No. 14.

Evangelii nuntiandi (On Evangelization in the Modern World). Apostolic exhortation of Pope Paul VI: December 8, 1975. No. 48.

Francis, Mark R. *Liturgy in a Multicultural Community.* Collegeville, Minnesota: The Liturgical Press, 1991.

García-Rivera, Alex. *St. Martin de Porres.* Maryknoll, New York: Orbis Books, 1995.

Goizueta, Roberto S. *Caminemos con Jesús: Toward a Hispanic/Latino Theology of Accompaniment.* Maryknoll, New York: Orbis Books, 1995.

Pérez Rodríguez, Arturo. *Popular Catholicism.* Washington, DC: The Pastoral Press, 1988.

Pérez Rodríguez, Arturo, Consuelo Covarrubias, and Edward Foley, eds. *Así Es: Stories of Hispanic Spirituality.* Collegeville, Minnesota: Liturgical Press, 1994.

Pineda, Ana Maria, and Schreiter, Robert, eds. *Dialogue Rejoined.* Collegeville, Minnesota: The Liturgical Press, 1995.

THE KISS OF PEACE:
A HISPANIC UNDERSTANDING
by Luis Vera, OSA, DMin

I n our own lives, we constantly experience transformation. This process repeatedly shapes and reshapes us, stretching our boundaries and horizons and trying to make us conscious of our very selves. In encountering ourselves as Christians, we also encounter the Holy. The desire for enduring peace is always present within all of us, especially in a society and a world that war has divided, for we are the people who "seek the face of the God of Jacob" (Psalm 24:6). I have been in North America for almost twenty years, and from the beginning my attention has been attracted to the way in which the Hispanic community shares the sign of peace in the Eucharistic liturgy.

One of the ways in which we Catholics celebrate who we are is through the liturgical life of the Church. It is through the liturgy "especially, that the faithful are enabled to express in their lives and manifest to others the mystery of Christ and the real nature of the true Church" (*Constitution on the Sacred Liturgy*, no. 2). We come to express ourselves as a gathered community and as a praying community. We not only celebrate but learn from one another as we create a large tapestry of peoples from different cultures and backgrounds, people who speak different languages and celebrate our faith in so many different ways. As we come together we become more who we are called to be.

Hispanics in the U.S. church

As a group, Hispanics are very different people because their realities are different. A Puerto Rican is different from a Mexican or a Cuban, and a Colombian from the south of Colombia is different from a Colombian from the east. Even though they speak basically the same language, they have their own idiosyncrasies because all share different histories and stories. Their narratives are diverse. Many times I have heard people from a non-Hispanic community saying that "the Hispanics do this or that" or "that's what they do," as if Hispanics would all do the same things, think the same way, and react in the same manner.

Though different Hispanic communities can be so different from each other, they also cherish many things in common. Hispanics are hopeful people. They are eschatological people, people who believe in the reign of God that is to come, "an eschatological community that lives, then, the hope of something beyond" (Romero, 22). It is difficult for the community to see that the reign of God is already present. For this reason Hispanics are people of Ash Wednesday and *Viernes Santo* (Good Friday). For Hispanics, it is difficult to see the joy of the Resurrection morning because that joy is not part of their immediate experience. Many of their countries live in a constant *Viernes Santo* and live and long to see the joy of the Resurrection. Many will never experience that "resurrection" in this life but in the life to come. Some experience that resurrection not on Easter morning but in the walking together as a community on the *Vía Crucis* (Way of the Cross). In this procession, they become one and experience the Christ of the Resurrection.

They also long to experience peace in their lives, not only spiritual but also physical peace. They value family life and community sharing, nourish their faith, and live in constant celebration. *La fiesta* is an important part of who they are. In the midst of suffering and death, in the midst of natural disasters and rejection, they celebrate. They celebrate because they believe in a better future. They celebrate because they realize that in difficulties they become one, and because they believe that *mañana será otro día* ("tomorrow will be another day"). They celebrate because a loving, compassionate God, a Mary who is always walking with them, and a family of saints who guides them always help them get through anything in life. This "extended family" will bring them peace and a better day, and so they celebrate.

Very often people complain or say of the expression of the sign of peace within the Eucharist in a "Hispanic" celebration: "It is too long," "it takes too much time," "people start walking all over the church," "it is too messy," "we lose focus," and many other comments. A look at history, and therefore at the different forms of this gesture throughout the ages, will offer some new insights and will help us understand and learn from this ritual in the way the Hispanic community in the United States celebrates it.

The ancient location of the kiss of peace
One of the first places that mention the exchange of the kiss of peace is in the *First Apology of Justin Martyr* from about 150 C.E. The section mentioning the kiss follows an account of a baptism at

Eucharist and reads: "Having ended the prayers we greet one another with a kiss" (Burghardt, 70). The preparation of the gifts follows. There is no mention of the kiss of peace during the Sunday Eucharist, but we assume it was the same. In the third century, Tertullian refers to the kiss of peace as the seal of prayer (*De oratione*, chapter 18). Within the celebration of Eucharist, the kiss was given at the end of the Liturgy of the Word:

> Then, the deacon calls out: "Greet one another; let us kiss one another." Don't take this kiss to be like the kiss friends exchange when they meet in the marketplace. This is something different; the kiss expresses a union of souls and is a plea for complete reconciliation. The kiss then, is a sign that our souls are united and all grudges banished. This is what our Lord meant when he said: "If you are offering your gift on the altar and remember there that your brother has a complaint against you, leave your gift on the altar and go first and be reconciled with your brother and then come and offer your gift" (Matthew 5:23–24). Thus the kiss is reconciliation, and so is holy, as blessed Paul implied when he proclaimed: "Greet one another with the kiss of charity" (Yarnold, 182–183).

The Apostolic Tradition of Hippolytus also mentions the kiss of peace at the ordination of a bishop before the presentation of gifts (Hyppolytus, 35).

In the Byzantine liturgy, "A sign of peace is exchanged at this point [before the Nicene Creed, which precedes the Eucharistic Prayer] by the priest at the altar. . . . The peace appears to have been exchanged by all present until some time between the ninth and eleventh centuries; it probably died out because a kiss upon the mouth, such as this was, would inevitably be stylized and modified" (Woolfenden, 243).

In the East, this exchange of the sign of peace remains before the Eucharistic Prayer, and the Eastern liturgy sees it as a preparation for the offering of the gifts and praying the Eucharistic Prayer by all those gathered. In the West we can also find similar actions. The Mozarabic rite, or the Spanish liturgy, which was the autonomous liturgy in constant use in Spain from the beginning of the sixth century until the Council of Braga suppressed it in 1080, is comparable to the Eastern rite in this matter. A lengthy formula for solemn intercessions and then the exchange of peace preceding the Eucharistic Prayer follow the transfer of the gifts. These intercessions "conclude with the sign of peace, ending with the song *Ad Pacem*, which immediately precedes the preface dialogue" (Lenti, 422). Saint Augustine refers to exchanging the peace after the Lord's Prayer, but he also expected the fraction to follow the Eucharistic Prayer and to precede the Lord's Prayer, and so the sign of peace led directly to Communion and not fraction (Woolfenden, 245).

Josef Jungmann mentions that "in the Carolingian era also the same succession (of kiss of peace and distribution of Communion) is found both at Communion of the sick and at public service. Indeed the kiss is often restricted to the communicants" (Jungmann, 481). He mentions that the *canones* of Theodore of Canterbury in the eighth century had in their rule: "Whoever does not communicate should not receive the [kiss of] peace nor the kiss in church" (481). Jungmann notices that elsewhere "the kiss of peace gradually became a sort of substitute for Communion" (481). According to Jungmann, only neighbors exchanged this kiss of peace, not every person.

It is clear that some of the early Christian communities were accustomed to exchanging this kiss of peace after the Liturgy of the Word and before the Liturgy of the Eucharist. Two different scripture passages are used in connection with the placement of the kiss of peace, and these scriptures help us interpret differing meanings for it, although always it points to unity in the body of Christ and is a ratification of the eucharistic action. When the kiss of peace follows the Liturgy of the Word, it puts into practice the injunction in Matthew 5:23–24, where we are to be reconciled with brother and sister before we present our gifts at the altar. In our present liturgy, the prayer just before the invitation to exchange the sign of peace clearly provides a context for this holy exchange: the risen Jesus' wish of peace for the disciples gathered in the upper room (see John 20:19–21).

In other early Christian communities, however, the kiss of peace preceded Communion. Woolfenden, drawing on the work of Bernard J. Lee, argues that "it is interesting that those who have made proposals for new forms of Eucharistic worship are united in seeing the sign of peace as a moment of peace and reconciliation before the preparation of the table and the Eucharistic Prayer" (Jungmann, 251). We must keep this diversity in mind, especially when we look at the exchange of the sign of peace the Hispanic community at a Eucharistic liturgy

Luis Vera, OSA, DMin

celebrates in which people from different countries—some of them in conflict among themselves—come together for worship.

Present location and the gesture

The first indication of the present location for the kiss of peace in Rome appeared in 416, when Pope Innocent I wrote to the bishop of Gubbio telling him that he should follow the Roman custom of having the kiss of peace at the end of the Eucharistic Prayer, because the bishop had been following the more ancient practice (Reese, 16). Today some wonder whether it is debatable that the priest exchange the sign of peace with only those in the sanctuary or go to the assembly to exchange it there. Some argue that he has already extended peace to the entire congregation ("The peace of the Lord be with you") and does not have to give it to individuals. But if this is the case, why does he exchange it with only those in the sanctuary?

Earlier sources (the *Ordines Romani*) suggest that the kiss of peace did not originate with the presider and then proceed in an orderly way to the rest of the assembly, but that each member of the clergy extended the sign of peace to his neighbor while the faithful extended it among themselves. Later formulations were made to start the kiss of peace from the altar to the people, i.e., like a message, handed from the presider to the others. The presider first kissed the altar, the missal, the crucifix, chalice, or the consecrated host before he extended the sign of peace to others. The people were to receive this gesture from the priest. Even when communicated among the assembly by the pax-board, which was a small tablet of wood, ivory, or metal with the figure of Christ, a saint, or a symbolic figure engraved or painted on it, it was understood that the peace first of all came from the priest. At different times both in the East and in the West, men and women in the assembly were separated; therefore, women gave the kiss of peace to women, men to men.

The "Sign of Peace" booklet the United States Conference of Bishops published in 1977 states: "It is also clear that the sign of peace is to be exchanged with persons who are rather close by (*General Instruction*, no. 112). Neither the people nor the ministers need try to exhaust the sign by attempting to give the greeting personally to everyone in the congregation or even to a great number of those present." What the 1970 *General Instruction of the Roman Missal* (*GIRM*) really says is: "All exchange some sign of peace and love, according to the local custom. The priest may give the sign of peace to the ministers." The statement from the bishops' conference is obviously interpreting something that does not seem to be that clear in the *Instruction*. This directive from the bishops' conference interprets that "the reason for this 'limited sharing' is that the priest has already prayed for peace among all present and has addressed them with words that are all inclusive: 'The peace of the Lord be with you always.' " The new *General Instruction of the Roman Missal* states: "As for the sign of peace to be given, the manner is to be established by Conferences of Bishops in accordance with the culture and customs of the peoples. It is, however, appropriate that each person offer the sign of peace only to those who are nearest and in a sober manner" (no. 82). In other words, the sign of peace is symbolic; giving it to a few is tantamount to giving it to the whole body of Christ.

The Constitution on the Sacred Liturgy (no. 50) asked for a careful examination of each part of the Eucharistic liturgy to be revised. The *Constitution* called for simplicity in adaptation to other cultures and stated that "other elements that have suffered injury through accident of history are now, as it may seem useful or necessary, to be restored to the vigor they had in the traditions of the Fathers." The sign of peace is one of those elements that had suffered injury and neglect throughout history. The kiss of peace in our liturgies occurs after the Lord's Prayer and before the breaking of the bread. The new *GIRM* reads: "The Rite of Peace follows, by which the church asks for peace and unity for herself and for the whole human family, and the faithful express to each other their ecclesial communion and mutual charity before communicating in the Sacrament" (no. 82).

Different meanings

A kiss can have many meanings depending on the persons who kiss, the place, the times, and the culture. It could be a sexual sign, a greeting, a good-bye, an expression of a special relationship, an act of aggression if it is not wanted, and even an act of betrayal (Judas) (Reese, 13). Some people say that it is a sign of reconciliation, especially after the Lord's Prayer: "Forgive us our trespasses, as we forgive those who trespass against us." Thomas Reese mentions that the sign of peace fulfills that prayer through an action, that is, we show our forgiveness to each other in a concrete, visual way; therefore, people bestow a blessing upon each other: "The peace of Christ be with you." People exchange it with smiles and joy, not with tears of regret. The sign of peace is not merely an expression of

Luis Vera, OSA, DMin

solidarity or good will; "it is rather an opening of ourselves and our neighbors to a challenge and a gift from beyond ourselves" (Reese, 14). In his letter to the Romans, Paul writes: "Greet one another with a holy kiss" (Romans 16:16; 1 Corinthians 16:20; 2 Corinthians 13:12; 1 Thessalonians 5:26). In other words, people understand this sign of peace in many different ways.

How Hispanics celebrate in the U.S.

Some say that most Hispanic Catholics in the United States have never heard about the Second Vatican Council. This implies that most Hispanic Catholics in this country are unaware of the liturgical reforms the Church called for in its decrees. Yet pastoral workers frequently note the vibrant and lively liturgical life of Hispanic communities. Hispanics, even without knowing it, are aware of a call to worship in the way those directives promoted (Matovina, 18–19).

Hispanics consider liturgical celebrations to be encounters with the person of Jesus. These encounters become alive, especially in celebrations such as *Viernes Santo* (Good Friday). On Good Friday the whole day is devoted to an encounter with the human Jesus in *Las Siete Palabras* (the Seven Last Words), the *Via Crucis* (the Way of the Cross), *el Santo Entierro* (the entombment), and, in some places like Puerto Rico and the Dominican Republic, *el Encuentro* (the encounter) or the procession of *La Dolorosa* (Our Mother of Sorrows). These celebrations bring Hispanics close to the human Jesus who has suffered in the same way they have. They are a recognition of the Christ who still lives among them and suffers with them. A Hispanic can laugh at difficulties, always waiting for justice and living in the hope of a better world.

For Hispanics, liturgies celebrate the "extended family" of God and therefore theirs, too. Here we direct our attention to the significance of the *padrinos* (godparents), who are selected not only for the sacraments of baptism and confirmation but also for marriages, First Communions, and the *quinceañeras* (fifteenth birthdays). Once the *padrinos* are chosen, they become *compadres* or co-parents. These *compadres* become part of the extended family and will share in caring for the well being and spiritual needs of the child or *ahijado/a*. One can also see this understanding of extended family in the way Mary and the saints are remembered. They become part of our human family. "The extended family grows and is created through symbolic and sacred moments of liturgy, blessings, fiestas, and *despedidas*—farewells. These are moments of color, song, dance and ritual" (Vela, 40). Their preference for "numerous statues and images in churches stems in large parts from this understanding of Liturgy as an extension of familial ties into the community of believers, both past and present" (ibid.). During the Sunday Eucharist, perhaps the only day during the week when people have the opportunity to see each other, they express those human bonds and the love that already exists among family members and friends and share with others in different ways. As people gather before and after Mass, the *saludos*, *besos, y abrazos* (greetings, embraces, and kisses) are very obvious.

Hispanics welcome people *con un beso y un abrazo* (with a kiss and an embrace). These feelings will continue and will find different forms of expression throughout most Spanish-language Eucharistic celebrations, and are often manifested at the kiss of peace. This orientation is a way of teaching others the meaning of church for the Hispanic community and how they express their own theology of community. On the other hand these expressions are more than only warm feelings, but are also a way of being and a way of including all members in an extended family. For Hispanics, family means not having to live, struggle, and dream alone, but *acompañados* (accompanied). They cannot see themselves in isolation, but always in relationship. Roberto Goizueta argues that "to be an isolated individual is, literally, to have no humanity, no identity, no self, it is to be no-thing, no-body" (Goizueta, 50). That *acompañamiento* (accompaniment) finds its place both at home and in the liturgy. As we accompany each other, we are also hospitable and welcoming.

A sense of hospitality and celebration

For Hispanics, hospitality is essential. They see a crucial virtue and an honor in extending hospitality to others but also in accepting that hospitality from others. They express and share it from the first moment they meet people. Even when there is a lack of *confianza* (trust), still to be hospitable is part of being a person. The "*mi casa es su casa* (my house is your house)" spirituality is a golden rule. In extending hospitality to others, the family circle is extended. Even though there are many differences among peoples, there are also common characteristics: the cultural value of the dignity of each person, the deep love and regard for the extended family, the celebration of life as a gift, e.g., *presentación* (presentation of a baby in the temple after birth), *tres añitos* (presentation of children in the temple when they turn three years old), *quinceañeras* (celebration of the fifteenth birthday), and many others. People like to savor their time as a gift to enjoy, not by themselves but with others. Hispanics share, one way or another, the sense of hospitality and the abiding faith that permeates their daily lives not only with those they know but even with the stranger. I remember my mother setting up another plate during dinner time "*por si álguien llega* (in case someone stops by)."

As they welcome others into their lives, they also welcome their "holy" family. Phrases that point to the divine are part of the vocabulary and expressions of Hispanics, e.g., "*Dios te bendiga* (May God bless you)," "*Si Dios quiere* (If God wills it)," "*Ay, Dios mío* (Oh, my God)," "*¡Santo Dios!* (Holy God)," "*Con Dios por delante* (With God before us)," "*Primero Dios* (God first)," and many others. Justo L. González mentions that "a new way of being Hispanic is being born in the United States. Being a Mexican-American is not the same as being a Mexican-American in Mexico" (González, 12). He argues that we "become partners in forging a new reality. . . . This reality, which some called 'Hispanic' and some call Latino, is currently being born . . . ." (13). In other words, living in the Unites States creates a different reality and a new identity.

Celebrations as well are essential for Hispanics as individuals and as a community. The social aspect of the sacraments has great importance, and it is unthinkable not to celebrate religious events. Sunday is the day when the family and the community gather precisely to do that: to celebrate. They come to church with their best clothes because they are going "*a la casa del Señor* (to God's house)"; therefore, one wears one's best for the Lord. Hispanics consider themselves good storytellers, and they come to hear the stories of their faith. Sharing food and drink also strengthen friendship and family ties. This aspect creates a wonderful opportunity and a great challenge to understand the Eucharist as essential to their lives.

What does the kiss of peace mean?

One could offer various reasons why the kiss of peace during the Eucharistic liturgy the U.S. Hispanic community celebrates is filled with so much enthusiasm, joy, and spontaneity. These reasons could become great elements for catechizing all our communities, but especially for creating a stronger sense of unity in diversity:

1. The kiss of peace increases the sense of family and extended family that is at the heart of the Hispanic/Latino community and ties all to a communion of worship.

2. It represents a concrete sign and tells of a future desire for peace and reconciliation among people. This waiting is not passive but one that leads to action and the constant struggle to overcome oppressive structures.

3. It is another moment during this holy celebration in which holy people can socialize and greet each other in a ritual way.

4. The sharing of the Body and Blood of Christ is the primordial sign of unity among the faithful, but because so many people do not receive Communion due to certain understandings, misunderstandings, and/ or different situations in their lives, the exchange of the sign of peace is a way in which that expression of unity occurs. Proper catechesis and religious instruction can address some of these difficulties. Some others are more difficult, for they involve other elements that very often are out of our reach, such as legal or immigration issues. The kiss of peace offers one moment of participation and acceptance for everyone. It is indeed a sign of common-union in which old and young, sinners and saints, broken and holy people become one in gesture and song, in hope and faith.

5. The exchange of the kiss of peace has become a sign of the identity of the Hispanic community living in the United States and a sign of hospitality. The community has become known in the U.S. for the way in which it shares the kiss of peace during the Eucharist, and for the way in which it has become a sign of unity and welcoming among different peoples.

Conclusion

If for Hispanics the kiss of peace is, among other things, a concrete sign of celebrating not only their identity as a U.S. church community but also of hospitality, then we might need to ask ourselves if these cultural elements support the current location of the rite or perhaps call for a change. Having the sign of peace in its present location might emphasize the reconciling nature of the gesture before receiving the Body and Blood of the Lord. Hispanics, however, teach us that we should extend hospitality from the very beginning of an encounter as the relationship is nourished and grows in many different ways. Should the community wait until the rite of Communion to express a sign of communal reconciliation? Do we wait until we bring and present our gifts of bread and wine? Our ecclesial experience teaches us that liturgy flourishes within a climate of hospitality. From the

_____ *Luis Vera, OSA, DMin*

welcoming environment outside the church building to the warm greeting by the ministers of hospitality at the gathering space where strangers become known to one another, the community experiences this hospitality.

Hospitality is nourished in the place where people sit together and where "the community worships as a single body united in faith, not simply as individuals who happen to find themselves in one place" (*Built of Living Stones*, no. 52), but as a *pueblo* (a people) who gather in worship and together invoke a community of Father, Son, and Holy Spirit. To try to formalize the expression of the sign of peace during the liturgical celebration of the Hispanic community in the U.S. may constrict an important expression of the faith of a community as well as the development of the identity of a people who are already strangers in a strange land. Catechesis must continue for everyone, and a conversation between the Hispanic community and the pastors of our churches must happen before we make any decisions or before we impose rules on the community.

As a community and as a people who walk by faith, Hispanics are eager to share their stories, and in the sharing of those stories, to share who they are. As the gathered Hispanic community celebrates its life in the liturgy, we realize that we can see liturgy as catechesis, but we also understand that liturgy goes beyond catechesis and helps us be and become more who we are and who we are called to be in the presence of God and of one another. There is a song that offers a prophetic vision for Hispanics living in the U.S.:

> *Sois la semilla que ha de creer,*
> *sois la estrella que ha de brillar.*
> *Sois levadura, sois grano de sal,*
> *Antorcha que debe alumbrar . . .*
> (Gabaráin)

> You are the seed that is to grow,
> you are the star that is to shine.
> You are the yeast, you are the salt,
> a torch that should give light . . .

May this community teach us and learn themselves that they are called to be seed, star, yeast, salt, torch . . . and peace.

References

Abbot, Walter M., ed. *The Documents of Vatican II*. London: Chapman, 1967.

Bishops' Committee on the Liturgy. *Built of Living Stones: Art, Architecture, and Worship*. Washington, DC: United States Catholic Conference, 2000.

Bishops' Committee on the Liturgy. "The Sign of Peace." Washington, DC: United States Catholic Conference, 1977.

Buckley, Francis. "Popular Religiosity and Sacramentality: Learning from Hispanics a Deeper Sense of Symbol, Ritual and Sacrament." *The Living Light* 27, no. 4 (Summer 1991): 351–360.

Burghardt, Walter J., John J. Dillon, and Dennis D. McManus, eds. Leslie William Banard, trans. *The First and the Second Apologies*, no. 65. New York/New Jersey: Paulist Press, 1997.

Francis, Mark R. "Hispanics, Popular Piety, and Liturgical Reform." *Modern Liturgy* 18, no. 8 (October 1991): 14–17.

Gabaráin, Cesáreo. "Id y Enseñad." In *Flor y Canto*. Portland, Oregon: Oregon Catholic Press, 1991.

Goizueta, Roberto S. *Caminemos con Jesús: Toward a Hispanic/Latino Theology of Accompaniment*. Maryknoll, New York: Orbis Books, 1992.

Goiuzeta, Roberto S. *We Are a People! Initiatives in Hispanic American Theology*. Minneapolis: Fortress Press, 1992.

Gómez, Raúl. "Professing Unity in Faith and Love: Hispano-Mozarabic Diptychs." *Liturgy* 13, no. 1 (1996): 60–63.

González, Justo L. "Hispanics in the United States." *Listening* 27, no. 1 (Winter 1992): 7–16.

González, Roberto, and Michael La Velle. *The Hispanic Catholic in the United States: A Socio-Cultural and Religious Profile*. New York: Northeast Catholic Pastoral Center for Hispanics, Inc., 1985.

Hyppolytus. *The Apostolic Tradition of Hippolytus*. Burton Scott Easton, trans. Hamden, Connecticut: Archon Books, 1962.

Jungmann, Josef A. *The Mass of the Roman Rite: Its Origins and Development*. Francis A. Brunner, trans. New York: Benzinger Brothers, Inc., 1959.

―――. "Generalities: Kiss of Peace." In *The Mass: An Historical, Theological, and Pastoral Survey*. Julian Fernandes, trans. Collegeville, Minnesota: The Liturgical Press, 1976, 209–211.

Lenti, Vincent A. "Liturgical Reform and the Ambrosian and

Mozarabic Rites." *Worship* 68, no. 5 (September 1994): 417–426.

Matovina, Timothy M. "U.S. Hispanic Catholics and Liturgical Reform." *America* 168, no. 13 (October 30, 1993): 18–19.

Pineda, Ana María. "Hispanic Identity." *Church* 4, no. 4 (Winter 1988): 51–55.

Reese, Thomas J. "In the Catholic Church, a Kiss Is Never Just a Kiss." *America* 172, no. 13 (April 15, 1995): 12–19.

Romero, Oscar. *Archbishop Oscar Romero: A Shepherd's Diary.* Irene B. Hodgson, trans. Cincinnati: St. Anthony Messenger Press and Novalis, 1995.

Taft, Robert F. *The Great Entrance.* Rome: Orientalia Christiana Analecta, 1975.

Vela, Rudy. "Hispanic Bienvenida—An Embrace and a Kiss." *Pastoral Music* (June–July 1989): 40.

Woolfenden, Graham. "Let Us Offer Each Other the Sign of Peace." *Worship* 67, no. 3 (May 1993): 239–252.

Yarnold, Edward. "Mystagogic Catechesis 5, #3." In *Cyril of Jerusalem.* London/New York: Routledge, 2000.

PART II

Liturgy & Devotions

LATINO/A SPIRITUALITY
AND THE UNIVERSAL CALL TO HOLINESS
Peter J. Casarella

An advertising slogan for a Hispanic television channel in southern Florida claims that the network is "as American as flan." This clever marketing technique reveals a new way to approach the Hispanic future of the United States. With the news that Hispanics have become the country's largest minority, it becomes all the more difficult to ignore the reality that underlies the results of a census. Even before the recent rancor about immigration reform began to grip the nation, the press in the United States had begun to pay more attention to the changing Hispanic population. The context for Hispanic ministry is changing. What was once commonly named "the Hispanic presence" lies at the juncture of divergent realities—a widespread recognition of a growing population that manifests considerable racial, ethnic, and economic diversity as well as increased anxiety about the visible presence of its undocumented and unassimilated members.

Even when this social transformation receives a favorable evaluation, both the Church and the larger society in the U.S. continue to disseminate falsehoods of various sorts. The prejudices cannot be attributed solely to the social blindness of non-Hispanics in the U.S. or to the success of proselytism by Pentecostals, even though both of these dynamics are prevalent (for a balanced treatment of the latter, see José Antonio Rubio, "Bearing False Witness," in *Cuerpo de Cristo*, 213–27).

Hispanic Catholics in the U.S. must also take stock of the new situation. Within our own community, one frequently encounters shortcomings in faith formation and a shocking ignorance of our own spiritual heritage.

The slogan "as American as flan" displays the genius of public relations. Perhaps the larger U.S. population will come to accept Latino/as, flan, and Telemundo in the way that they accept piñatas or home run kings from the Caribbean. The challenge Hispanic Catholics face in the domain of religious identity is quite distinct from that of marketing. A spiritual heritage is ultimately not a commodity that can be bought or sold, for it presupposes a reality an entire people take to heart.

Even public recognition does not suffice to establish a tradition. For example, in 1997 the U.S. Postal Service paid homage to Father Félix Varela as a social reformer and journalist. The government honored Varela by creating a 32-cent stamp bearing his image. One does not slight the cultural value of such civic recognition by noting that buying a stamp and grasping the total impact of a follower of Christ are two separate matters.

Who was Father Félix Varela (1788–1853)? He was a Cuban philosopher who escaped to New York City after a threat of persecution by the Spanish crown forced him to flee his homeland and Spain. While in New York, he was recognized as a champion of the new Irish immigrants whom an upsurge of anti-Catholicism threatened. Varela is just one example of prophetic Hispanic Catholics (see Mario T. García, "Catholic Social Doctrine and Mexican American Political Thought," in *Cuerpo de Cristo*, 292–311). There are no "experts" in the path to holiness. What we encounter in the witness of holy women and men is a concrete life. This model can help believers respond in their own way to the universal call to holiness. In such figures we see the point of intersection of the traces of Christ's own love for humanity etched into the plane of human history. Exploring the Christian past is no longer the work of committing facts and dates to memory. What counts in our exploration of the past is the encounter with real women and men of faith.

The Hispanic presence as a blessing and a prophetic witness

The expanding presence of Latinos and Latinas in the U.S. requires a new approach to pastoral ministry. Some in the Church believe that the "problem" of the Hispanic presence will ultimately resolve itself. I am not referring to overt antagonism to Hispanic congregations, Masses, or fellow parishioners. I am referring to well-meaning proponents of Hispanic assimilation. Such persons assume that the new influx will accommodate itself to the pattern of "Americanization" that Western European Catholics underwent in the first half of the twentieth century. For such Catholics the new demographic explosion will not mean any major modifications to the face of U.S. Catholicism nor its forms of expression (see Charles Morris, *American Catholics*). Seen from this perspective, the phenomenon of Mass in Spanish or other pastoral initiatives that serve Hispanic parishioners are merely provisional. The dominant model of the parish, its style of celebrating

_____ *Peter J. Casarella*

the Mass, and other aspects of this paradigm will return in one or two generations once the current wave of immigrants is incorporated into the mainstream. In this view the Hispanic presence represents no more than a current obstacle to pastoral planning.

What the U.S. Catholic bishops wrote in their 1984 document on the Hispanic presence radically opposed the model of assimilation. The bishops began with these words (which are repeated in another document published eleven years later): "In this moment of grace we recognize that the Hispanic presence in our midst is a blessing from God" (*The Hispanic Presence*).

There is a big difference between thinking of the Hispanic presence as a pastoral problem and thinking of it as a blessing from God. The view that looks beyond assimilation is confirmed by the prophetic words of Pope John Paul II in his letter to Bishop Roberto González:

> Based on their rich history and their experience, the Hispanic community can offer a unique contribution to the dialogue between faith and culture in current U.S. society and in this way can open new paths to carry forward the Gospel into the third millennium (*Hispanic Presence*, Letter to Bishop Roberto González, May 8, 1995).

In a culture in which cultural Protestantism and secularism hold sway, the Catholic culture of U.S. Hispanics should not be underestimated (*Hispanic Presence*, 32). For the bishops it is not a matter of promoting *la raza* or *hispanidad* as such. The task of proclaiming the gospel transcends all races and all cultural manifestations of faith. To put it another way: Hispanic culture possesses virtues that promote an authentic disposition of faith, but no culture by itself (Hispanic or Anglo-Saxon) is identical to the gift of grace that leads to Jesus Christ. The essential contribution of Hispanic Catholics, which the bishops call "a providential resource" in the task of evangelization, is rooted in the domain of faith and culture.

The preferential love for the poor and for recently arrived immigrants belongs integrally to this vision of faith. This form of solidarity contributes to the political dimension of the call to holiness. As a consequence the bishops affirm that the Hispanic presence is a "prophetic warning." In their words, "If Hispanic Catholics . . . are not offered a place in the church in which they feel at home, the loss of their Catholic identity will be a serious blow to the church in our country." The political parties in the U.S. have not grasped that the Hispanic Catholic is by nature a *paradox*. The typical Hispanic voter shares the social values and pro-family stance of political conservatives and also shares with progressives the view that the state should commit its resources to lend support to the poorest and to immigrants in need. Seen in these terms, the everyday reality of Hispanic Catholics cannot be translated into either the liberal or the conservative social idiom that dominates U.S. culture today (cf. John Francis Burke, *Mestizo Democracy*). Hispanics can and must keep speaking their own language, not only in the literal sense but also in the more extended sense of upholding the virtues of their community and their own style of life.

The language of sanctity

The National Pastoral Plan for Hispanic Ministry, a document the U.S. bishops approved in 1987, uses the term *la mística Hispana* or what may also be termed Latino/a spirituality. It extends beyond the scope of this essay to examine the difference between *la mística* and "spirituality" from the perspective of Latinos and Latinas. (Gilberto Cavazos-González, OFM, has explored the question of how the U.S. Latino/a experience requires its own inculturated spirituality in a *New Theology Review* article entitled "*Cara y Corazón* [Face and Heart]: Toward a U.S. Latino Spirituality of Inculturation.") But in the context of the bishops' document from 1987 this potentially rich term remains vague and undefined. What the bishops took in 1987 to be self-evident requires greater clarification.

Since 1987 the U.S. bishops and Rome have published many more documents that allude to the Hispanic presence. On the level of the universal church one could also mention the documents of the Jubilee Year 2000 and the post-synodal apostolic letter *Ecclesia in America*. (On the latter see my "Solidarity as the Fruit of Communio: *Ecclesia in America*, 'Post-Liberation Theology,' and the Earth," *Communio: International Catholic Review* 27 [Spring 2000]: 98–123.) I base what follows on the apostolic letter *Novo Millenio Ineunte* and a speech John Paul II delivered in April of 2001.

Novo Millenio Ineunte was written to introduce the message of Christ to the third millennium of Christian history. The pontiff is quite clear in stating: "First of all, I have no hesitation in saying that all pastoral initiatives must be set in relation to *holiness* (no. 30)." (The term *santidad* can be translated into English as either "holiness" or "sanctity." The former, I think, resonates better with those who belong to Christian traditions that emphasize the inward renewal of the individual and the latter with traditions that elevate such individuals in a public way to the status of official veneration. The real point is to see that *santidad* in the imitation of Christ is a personal bridge between the transformation of the isolated heart and the social witness of the Church.) But the Holy Father also recognized that pastoral initiatives undertaken in relation to holiness cannot be preprogrammed:

> At first glance, it might seem almost impractical to recall this elementary truth as the foundation of the pastoral planning in which we are involved at the start of the new millennium. Can holiness ever be "planned"? What might the word "holiness" mean in the context of a pastoral plan? (no. 31)

In light of this challenge, is it even possible to "implement" a universal call to holiness on the level of pastoral planning? The starting point is the awareness that all Christians are called to the way of sanctity:

> This ideal of perfection must not be misunderstood as if it involved some kind of extraordinary existence, possible only for a few "uncommon heroes" of holiness. The ways of holiness are many, according to the vocation of each individual (ibid.).

The pedagogy of personal holiness must adapt itself to the rhythms of an individual's existence. In other words, there is no recipe for holiness. The Church beatifies or canonizes people not only for their heroic deeds (which can often be obvious and numerous) but also for the ways in which these holy women and men have applied the gifts of the Holy Spirit to their daily lives.

The number of examples of holiness that the Church has called to our attention has grown rapidly in recent years. Consider, for example, the new doctor of the Church, Saint Thérèse of Lisieux (*La Teresita*), or blessed Father Mariano de Jesús Hoyos (Don Marianito), a Colombian priest from the beginning of the twentieth century. More recently, Pope Benedict XVI beatified José Anacleto González Flores (also known as the "Mexican Gandhi") and his eight companions. These men were martyrs of the bloody Cristero War in Mexico from 1926 to 1929 and displayed exemplary Christian fortitude as well as reverence for the Eucharist, a firm devotion to the Blessed Mother, and a willingness to pray for their executioners. (The beatification took place on November 15, 2005. For more information about the holiness of these martyrs, see *http://www.vatican.va/news_services/liturgy/saints/ns_lit_doc_20051120_anacleto-gonzalez_en.html* [accessed on September 4, 2006]).

Being a saint is a matter of loving as our Lord taught us to love: "To imitate the holiness of God, as it was made manifest in Jesus Christ his Son, 'is nothing other than to extend in history his love, especially towards the poor, the sick and the needy' " (*Ecclesia*, no. 31, citing Luke 10:25). The universal vocation to holiness presupposes a change of heart, a *metanoia* ("conversion"), in the language of the New Testament. This transformation takes place not only on the level of the intellect but comprises a renewal of one's way of life based upon the criteria set forth in the gospel (*Ecclesia*, no. 26). "Faith that works through love" (Galatians 5:6) is essential to genuine conversion. Asceticism, to the degree that it does not become an end unto itself, can also promote conversion. This total conversion leads us to a new life in which

> the gap between faith and life must be bridged. Where this gap exists, Christians are such only in name. To be true disciples of the Lord, believers must bear witness to their faith, and witnesses testify not only with words, but also with their lives. . . . The greatest witness is martyrdom (ibid.).

Catholics recognize that encounter can take place in the prayerful reading of scripture, through the reception of the sacraments, and in the communal experience of the people of God. In the process, however, the Lord does not hide his face. His love endures and offers encouragement through each stage of our individual commitments. He is *encountered*.

In order to develop a pastoral plan in relation to holiness, we have to learn the "language of sanctity" and be able to translate this language in highly diverse contexts. It appears that Pope John Paul II coined this expression in a speech he gave to Spanish-speaking pilgrims in Rome attending the beatification of Carlos Manuel Rodríguez Santiago, the first Puerto Rican elevated to the glory of the altars and a man affectionately known as "Charlie" (cf. *Tertio Millennio Adveniente*, no. 37 on the "ecumenical eloquence" of the saints). In the pope's words: "In fact, the Church fully expresses her universal mission when she speaks the language of holiness and especially when she must adopt this language in the contemporary age, in which the Spirit spurs her to a renewed proclamation of the Gospel in every corner of the earth" (from the beatification ceremony of April, 30, 2001. See *www.vatican.va/holy_ father/john_paul_ii/speeches/2001/documents/hf_jp-ii_spe_20010430_ beatificazione_en.html* [accessed on September 4, 2006] for full text).

The idea that sanctity is a kind of discourse has great relevance to the Hispanic community in the U.S. Each Hispanic has his or her own national background, Marian devotion, and unique path. As a result, the path to holiness among recently arrived Latinos and Latinas will be one that requires a new language of faith suited to the new context. No one will be forced in the process to abandon the traditions or devotions of one's country of origin, and everyone has the obligation to respect and welcome the traditions of other Hispanics.

There is no single expression of Hispanic popular religion that shares *all* the traditions of Spanish-speaking lands. Diverse Latino/a customs have become mixed together in the new reality of the United States. For that very reason pastoral agents have much to gain by paying attention to the language of sanctity as a possession Hispanics hold in common. Speaking the language of sanctity is a way to uphold a Catholic common ground within our own community of faith.

Father Félix Varela as a follower of Christ

I think that the model of *sequela Christi* ("the following of Christ") that the life and thought of Father Varela offered is of great relevance to the situation of Hispanics in the U.S. today. During his visit to Cuba in 1998, Pope John Paul II often made reference to Varela. It is not hard to understand why the bishop of Rome would recall the figure of Varela in this setting. Varela is known as the "one who taught Cubans how to think," and no small part of that legacy was his ardent defense of personal freedom. As an elected official of the Spanish *Cortes* (legislature) in Cádiz, Varela proposed a defense of the rights of the slaves, and for that stance was for all intents and purposes exiled to

New York City. As a parish priest in the United States, he helped the poor and utilized his considerable erudition to defend the national identity of the new Irish immigrants. After being named vicar general of New York, he participated in 1837 as a theologian at the Synod of Baltimore. Throughout the period of his exile, he continued to be admired as a man of letters, and he dedicated himself to developing a Christian foundation for a view of tolerance that would apply to the whole American continent.

Can one actually speak of a distinctively Varelian spirituality? (This topic was examined in a brilliant dissertation that is regrettably hard to access from this country: Felipe J. Estévez, *Spirituality of Félix Varela: An Historical-Spiritual Study of Félix Varela's Pastoral Services to the Catholic Church in the United States 1825–1853*, Pontificia Universitas Gregoriana, Roma, 1980; what follows is drawn in part from the condensed version: Felipe J. Estévez, *El Perfil Pastoral de Félix Varela*, Miami: Ediciones Universal, 1989.) This spirituality includes at least three essential characteristics. A first trait was Varela's passion for the truth. He defended poor Catholic immigrants who arrived from Ireland. His writings, above all the two volumes of his *Letters to Elpidio* and his essays in the newspaper *El Habanero* derive from the anti-Catholic crusades of mid-nineteenth century America. He fought superstition with the same conviction that he demonstrated the reasonableness of Catholic thought and faith.

A second characteristic is his conception of the Church as the Mystical Body of Christ. In light of the fact that this biblical motif would become commonplace in Catholic thought one century later, Varela appears to be ahead of his times as a theologian as well. He promoted the reality of the Mystical Body through his apostolate with the poor, alcoholics, and orphans. In his life the face of Christ became visible in the face of the poor. When Varela wrote that the Church is a mystery of faith and charity, he was not referring to an abstract reality. For Father Varela, in the midst of the poor, the body of Christ had flesh and blood.

The third characteristic of Varela's witness has to do with the relationship of faith and freedom. He believed and fought to show that faith and freedom sustain one another. Rather than posit their incompatibility, Varela argued that impiety destroyed the establishment of a tolerant society. The practice of tolerance in a free society requires a religious foundation. Civil liberty thus comes to be seen as a gift from God. For Varela it is God's will that we treat the other as one who possesses an absolute dignity. Although Father Varela was a man deeply rooted in the intellectual currents and social conflicts of nineteenth-century America, his witness continues to teach Latinos and Latinas today to forge a new American identity for the new millennium.

Liturgy, popular piety, and the universal path to holiness

Father Félix Varela has not been declared a saint, but his followers (who included Pope John Paul II) find in him signs of the holiness of Christ. There is thus no need to put holy women and men on a pedestal in order to learn about Christ from their examples. The universal path to sanctity is a path anyone can follow. I will conclude this essay with a reflection on how this universal path lies at the intersection of liturgy and popular piety.

This fascinating and important topic has received renewed attention of late (see, for example, Peter Phan, ed., *Directory on Popular Piety and the Liturgy: Principles and Guidelines: A Commentary*, Collegeville, Minnesota: Liturgical Press, 2005, as well as the relevant essays in *Cuerpo de Cristo*). The much-cited statement on this question from the Second Vatican Council goes straight to the heart of the matter:

> Popular devotions of the Christian people are to be highly commended, provided they accord with the laws and norms of the Church, above all when they are ordered by the Apostolic See. . . . But these devotions should be so drawn up that they harmonize with the liturgical seasons, accord with the sacred liturgy, are in some fashion derived from it, and lead the people to it, since, in fact, the liturgy by its very nature far surpasses any of them (*Constitution on the Sacred Liturgy*, no. 13).

This passage reiterates a central theme of the Council, namely, that the liturgy is the source and summit of the Christian life. At the same time, it recognizes that the people of God can and should practice "popular devotions" in such a way as to uphold the priority of the liturgy. There was no intention here to prune away legitimate practices of faith, but one can see on balance a hint of suspicion that the popular devotions the people of God practiced could deviate from an authentically Catholic way of expressing the faith. There is nothing wrong with imposing prudent restrictions upon practices that depart from the faith of the Church, but a one-sided approach that also creates a generic predisposition to disparage all forms of popular Catholicism will not do.

The *Directory on Popular Piety and the Liturgy: Principles and Guidelines* from 2001 offers guidance on the specific question of how to interpret the teaching of the Council. The *Directory* is unequivocal about the need to maintain a proper balance between liturgy and popular piety:

> Thus, it is important that the question of the relationship between popular piety and the Liturgy not be posed in terms of contradiction, equality or, indeed, of substitution. A realization of the primordial importance of the Liturgy, and the quest for its most authentic expressions, should never lead to neglect of the reality of popular piety, or to a lack of appreciation for it, nor any position that would regard it as superfluous to the Church's worship or even injurious to it (no. 50).

The *Directory* offers guidelines for pastoral agents to make judgments regarding whether popular devotions are in actual concord with "the primordial importance of the liturgy." (The central concern seems to be the preservation of the centrality of the Paschal Mystery of our Lord in all pious exercises of faith. This criterion accords rather well with the focus on the crucified embrace of the Lord in Latino/a popular Catholicism; see, for example, my article as well as the book by Roberto S. Goizueta cited below.) More importantly, the *Directory* includes statements that could help to lift the veil of suspicion that obscured the evangelizing potential of popular devotions: "For its part, popular piety, because of its symbolic and expressive qualities, can often provide the Liturgy with important insights for inculturation and stimulate an effective dynamic creativity" (*Directory*, no. 58, citing the Puebla document discussed below).

The *Directory* also recognizes other authoritative sources for guidance on the matter that emanated from the Apostolic See and regional episcopal conferences (no. 2). In this regard, it is extremely important to recall the historic 1979 meeting in Puebla of the Latin American bishops with Pope John Paul II. In the bishops' document, they treat the relationship between *religiosidad popular* (popular Catholicism, popular piety) and evangelization in terms of their ability to complement one another. They specifically cite the need to recognize the pastoral task of "promoting the cross-fertilization (*mutua fecundación*) between liturgy and popular piety in order to be able to channel with lucidity and prudence the deep desire for prayer and charismatic vitality that today is being experienced in our countries" (*Third General Conference of CELAM*, Puebla, 1979, no. 465).

Latinos and Latinas in the U.S. also maintain a fervent devotion to the cult of saints. Much could be said about the public dimension of this devotion and especially the diverse processions that bring Latino/a popular piety into the streets of many urban settings in the U.S. (See, for example, my essay "The Painted Word," *The Journal of Hispanic/Latino Theology* 6 [November 1998]: 18–42.) But the relationship between the universal call to holiness and the official theology of the saints is also epitomized by a vignette recounted at an academic gathering by the saintly Cuban bishop from Miami, Agustín Román (the story is taken from Raúl R. Gómez, sds, "Veneration of the Saints and *Beati*," in Phan, ed., *Directory*, 121–22).

Bishop Román recounts how a young mother and her daughter enter a local church and gaze with admiration at the stained glass depictions of individual saints. When a catechist in the same parish later asks the girl about the identity of the saints, the child blurts out: "The saints, the saints, the saints are the windows of the church!" After considerable laughter at the child's naiveté, the little girl offers a startlingly apposite explanation: "The saints are the windows through which the light of Christ enters the church." The anecdote and visual image reveal how the saints—official and unofficial—inform the life of the faithful. To situate the life of holiness equally in the everyday sphere of domesticity and in the public liturgical life of the Church is no diminishment of the role of the parish or liturgy in the Christian life. On the contrary, following the holy women and men of God leads one ineluctably into the sanctuary of the church for both private and public prayer. We invoke and partake of the communion of saints in the Eucharist because we know they accompany us on the daily journey of faith.

The universal path to holiness is *un camino*. The notion of *un camino* appears in countless hymns Hispanic Catholics sing and which one can translate into English as "path." The Spanish word, however, maintains better than any translation a direct link to the act of walking (i.e., *caminar*). (This point is basic to the argument of Roberto S. Goizueta's book *Caminemos con Jesús*.) Walking through a city is a very different experience from taking a bus or battling traffic in one's own vehicle. When you walk, you are easily distracted. When you walk on the street, you are accompanied whether you like it or not by the poor, the elderly, those hurrying home from a night shift, and many others. Taking a walk is a very public act.

Félix Varela and other holy women and men of God teach us how to walk with Christ. In this respect, it is important to recall the lesson from the New Testament regarding the "way" Christ showed his followers, for the Greek term (*hodos*) the New Testament writers used conveys the dual sense of a concrete road and a path of learning (cf. John 14:6; Acts 16:17; 18:25; 18:26). There is a path to Christ in the Church because Christ is the path of the Church. Holy women and men of God illuminate this path and help us to follow to the Lord.

This essay represents an expanded version of my earlier piece "La Mística Hispana: ¿Un nuevo camino a la santidad en los Estados Unidos?" The original essay appeared in Amen: Una publicación del Instituto Nacional Hispano de Liturgia *1,4 no. 2 (Fall 2001): 12–15.*

References

Burke, John Francis. *Mestizo Democracy: The Politics of Crossing Borders*. College Station, Texas: Texas A&M University Press, 2002.

Casarella, Peter J. "Solidarity as the Fruit of Communio: *Ecclesia in America*, 'Post-Liberation Theology,' and the Earth." *Communio: International Catholic Review* 27 (Spring 2000): 98–123.

———. "The Painted Word." *The Journal of Hispanic/Latino Theology* 6 (November 1998): 18–42.

Casarella, Peter J., and Raúl Gómez, SDS, eds. *Cuerpo de Cristo: The Hispanic Presence in the U.S. Catholic Church*. New York: Crossroad, 1998.

Cavazos-González, Gilberto, OFM. "*Cara y Corazón* (Face and Heart): Toward a U.S. Latino Spirituality of Inculturation." *New Theology Review* 17 (May 2004): 46–55.

Estévez, Felipe J. *El Perfil Pastoral de Félix Varela*. Miami: Ediciones Universal, 1989.

Goizueta, Roberto S. *Caminemos con Jesús: Towards a Hispanic/Latino Theology of Accompaniment.* Maryknoll, New York: Orbis, 1995.

Morris, Charles. *American Catholics: The Saints and Sinners Who Built America's Most Powerful Church.* New York: Times Books, 1997.

National Conference of Catholic Bishops. *The Hispanic Presence in the New Evangelization in the United States,* bilingual edition. Washington, DC: NCCB, 1996.

Phan, Peter, ed. *Directory on Popular Piety and the Liturgy: Principles and Guidelines: A Commentary.* Collegeville, Minnesota: Liturgical Press, 2005.

CARLOS MANUEL:
APOSTLE OF THE NEW EVANGELIZATION
AND THE SANCTITY OF THE LAITY
Sr. Dominga Maria Zapata, SH

O n July 7, 1997, the process began for the Church's first-ever official recognition of the sanctity of a Caribbean layperson, Carlos Manuel Rodríguez Santiago. He is the second layperson in the Americas recognized for his holiness. Juan Diego was the saint at the beginning of the evangelization on the continent. Carlos Manuel leads us to an appreciation of the role of the laity in the new evangelization.

Pope John Paul II's declaration of 1987 as the Year of the Laity, calling the laity to a life of sanctity, inspired the beginning of Carlos Manuel's canonization cause. Carlos Manuel was declared Blessed on April 29, 2001. "Chali," as his family affectionately called him and as the people of Puerto Rico now know him, decided to follow Christ as a layperson to the end of his life.

Ordinarily, liturgy has been considered the field of the clergy and professional theologians within the Church. The laity was to attend or participate in it. Carlos Manuel's life offers a unique dimension of the vocation of the laity in relation to liturgy. His life and ministry were centered on Christ as lived through the worship of the church. Liturgy was the way he lived the mysteries of salvation and practiced his ministry so that others may know and live them deeply. As someone who lived before the Second Vatican Council's renewal of the liturgy, he was ahead of his times as a layperson.

Ordinary life in extraordinary ways

Carlos Manuel lived an ordinary life in an extraordinary Christian way. He was born in Caguas, Puerto Rico on November 22, 1918, into a family of five children. One of his sisters became a Carmelite sister and his only brother a Benedictine priest. Carlos Manuel's vocation as a layperson took the form of a total commitment to God. In complete identification with Christ, he centered his life on the Paschal Mystery. "*Vivimos para esta noche*" was the phrase that best described his zeal for the Paschal Mystery as the center and summit of the liturgy of the Church. Through the liturgy, Carlos Manuel was able to find the inseparable relationship between Christ and the Church.

God manifested Chali's calling very early in life. At the age of 13 Carlos Manuel contracted ulcerative colitis that would ultimately develop into cancer. His physical illness was part of his "dark night of faith" before he died on July 13, 1963, at the age of 45. His family testified to his acceptance of his illness without complaint. In addition, Chali did not use his illness as a reason or an excuse not to fulfill his call to sanctity in ordinary life.

He lived around the liturgical life of the Church. He became an eager reader of the Church's liturgical and scriptural documents in order to become a herald of their contents in life, even before Vatican II. He founded the publication *Cultura Cristiana* before *inculturation* was part of the Catholic vocabulary. In his ministry with university students, Chali, moved by the Holy Spirit, translated the formulas of the missal and other resources so that the students could follow the mysteries of God in a deeper way. He was a prophet for the use of the vernacular in the liturgical celebrations of the Church so that the people would understand and appreciate the meaning of what was celebrated. To further help people with understanding the liturgical celebrations and the Divine Office he founded *Liturgia*.

His devotion to the Blessed Virgin Mary, whom he called his *Theotocos*, was another means of support to his spiritual life. But Carlos Manuel's main source of spiritual nourishment was the Eucharist. Everything in the liturgical life of the Church led him to see and encounter the God who became human so we could become divine. "*La Vigilia Pascual es centro y meta de nuestra liturgia. Vivimos para esa Noche. ¡Aleluya!*" ("The Paschal Vigil is the center and goal of our liturgy. We live for that night. Alleluia!" [editor's translation]) But like Christ, Carlos Manuel had to suffer the Passion, physically and spiritually, before surrendering to the great "Exultet" for all eternity.

Before the Church's emphasis on the sanctity of the laity, Carlos Manuel modeled it for those to follow. He was convinced of his own phrase: "*La salvación del mundo depende del santo que yo llegue a ser. La santidad no es una especialización: es la vida cristiana toda la vida, todas las vibraciones del alma, todos los instantes de una existencia dignificada por la gracia de Cristo* ("The salvation of the world depends on the saint that I will become. Sanctity is not a specialization: It is the Christian life in its fullness, in all the movements of the soul, all the instances of a dignified existence through Christ's grace" [author's translation]) (*Novena al Beato Carlos M. Rodríquez Santiago*). One can see and touch such sanctity when one contemplates the eyes and gentle smile of Carlos Manuel's beatification picture.

The novena for Carlos Manuel manifests not only his sanctity of life but that which all Christians are called to show in their own lives. Each day of the novena invites us to contemplate a virtue and pray for the grace to live that virtue in our own life. As we meditate and pray the novena, we can encounter Carlos Manuel as a man of interior and exterior *peace*; of *fraternity* toward all sons and daughters of God, especially the poor, the humble, and simple; of *total surrender* to divine Providence, trusting God for all his needs; of deep *hope* as his guiding path toward sanctity and his constant message to all; of *pure heart* and tender spirit ready to forgive and be forgiven; of *solidarity* with the neighbor, especially those in need, that identified him as the "just one" who will enter the kingdom of God; of *patience*, especially toward the needy, the sick, children, and youth; of *kindness*, humility, and simplicity, always doing good; and of many blessings, especially the gift of healing and the power to perform miracles, stemming from his deep *prayer life* (from the *Novena*).

Pope John Paul II's apostolic exhortation *Christifideles Laici* invited the laity to become conscious of their gift and responsibility for the communion and mission of the Church. This call directly followed the thrust of Vatican II. Carlos Manuel, ahead of his times, responded fully to this call of the church with a deep awareness of being a true member of the Mystical Body of Christ. How was it possible that a sick person, with no professional theological studies, without any official ecclesiastical ministerial job, and without much encouragement from the body of the Church, became such a saintly model of Christian life? Where did this blessing begin?

As with every Christian, Carlos Manuel received a call at baptism, which his family nurtured and suffering purified. "*Il Illo Tempore* (at that time)," the Church remained "*a espaldas del pueblo*," ("with its back to the people" [editor's translation]) as was the symbol at Mass. There were many developments in Puerto Rico as well as all over the world. The 1950s marked an era of change from agricultural to an industrial society in Puerto Rico and its establishment as an *Estado Libre Asociado* (commonwealth status). A significant emigration to the mainland United States accompanied this development. Education, mass media, the end of the Korean War, the beginning of the Cold War, a new hope for developing countries through the support of the

United Nations, European recovery from the Second World War, the U.S. civil rights movement that Martin Luther King Jr. headed, Castro's victory in Cuba, communism as well as capitalism in the midst of secularism, improved health and life spans, and other developments all occurred during the last decades of Carlos Manuel's life. These events existed side by side with the dominant evils of the times: persistent poverty and misery for many, the increase of marginalized groups, high incidence of mental illness and emotional instability, demographic realities and the birth control response, and massive world immigration and displacement of families. Carlos Manuel could have lost hope in the midst of all these concerns. He was not isolated from the world. It was precisely his concern for the reality of the world that his faith led him to center his life in Christ as the only hope and solution to the problems of the world. How aware he was of the need to depend on holiness for true change!

Carlos Manuel's illness prevented him from following an ordinary course of studies but not from developing his intellectual gifts. He became a tireless reader, including works in Latin and English. His daily work as an office clerk provided Chali with enough money for his expenses, and whatever was left he would give to the poor. He traveled to work every day on public transportation in peaceful silence. He concretized his vocation in real life. There is no documentation that he ever wanted to become a priest or that he had made a vow of celibacy. What is clear is that he participated fully in the priesthood of Christ and remained faithful to celibacy as a single lay Christian (from *Un Santo Puertorriqueño*).

Carlos Manuel was open to all that God provided in his path to sanctity. Perhaps the influence liturgy had on him came from his contact with the Benedictines in Humacao, whom his brother had joined. The spirit of the Jesuits influenced him just as much through his work with Father Antonio G. Quevedo, SJ, at the Centro Universitario Católico in Rio Piedras, Puerto Rico. This last connection manifested itself through Carlos Manuel's true sense of obedience and his great desire always to think with the Church. Chali did more intense ministry during the tenure of Archbishop Jaime P. Davis, Archbishop of San Juan from 1943 to 1969. Archbishop Davis supported biblical and liturgical studies as well as pastoral ministry and university centers. He combined well the spiritual and the social ministries of the Church. All these influences created the proper setting for the development and commitment of a lay saint ahead of his times.

Carlos Manuel's sanctity was not based on merely natural characteristics of a committed person. While shy, once in front of a group he spoke with authority of the things that mattered the most to him and his relationship with Christ. Weakened by his illness, he nonetheless found strength to pray for hours each night and the Divine Office seven times a day, participate in daily Mass, meet weekly with the Liturgical Circle, write weekly articles and letters, conduct days of reflection on Christian life, learn to play the piano almost on his own, and enjoy family life. Above all Carlos Manuel found his strength and motivation for life in Christ.

Carlos Manuel lived his life attentive to the will of God for him in ordinary life. Yet he sought the graces God provided him and the means the Church offered to live life in extraordinary ways. Here lay the secret of sanctity. It is not a matter of the state of life of the Christian but rather the fidelity to God's call to follow Christ. Carlos Manuel found the center of his life in and through the celebration of the mysteries of salvation Christ brought about and gave to the body of Christ, the Church, to maintain before the world. He made the saints his best friends, especially those who offered a unique way to love the poor and have a mystical relationship with Christ as well as those who had converted to Christ. The source of sanctity in the Church was Carlos Manuel's life: liturgical life, all forms of prayer life, and the service of others. His seemed to have the wisdom to know Christ as Saint Paul did—not because he lived with Jesus but because God had chosen him to know Christ in order to bring him to others!

He had the privilege of understanding the meaning of the liturgical celebrations of the passion, death, and resurrection of Christ. He was able to further his Catholic formation through his capacity to read Latin and English publications. He was conscious that his faith commitment was not completed with liturgical celebrations in the temple, but that it necessarily had to overflow into life and into relationship with others, especially the poor and marginalized.

Chali was born and raised in a practicing Catholic family, but he did not hesitate to assume the responsibility to form his family further. Chali initiated the family into the use of the missal to follow the Latin Mass so they could to understand what the liturgy was celebrating. He gave them a short version of the Divine Office to encourage praying with the psalms. He was able to integrate the popular religiosity that was so much a part of his family and culture. His grandmother was a real model of sanctity through her charity and prayerful life. Chali inherited his grandmother's altar, where he continued to pray all his life, especially for hours after coming home from the liturgical celebrations of Christmas and Easter. His brother Pepe claimed Chali influenced him in the former's Benedictine vocation. All these facts contradict the belief that no one is a prophet in one's own house! Pepe was convinced that Carlos Manuel fulfilled his vocation, his mission in life, and his specific apostolate of announcing the Easter joy of salvation through Christ's death and resurrection without even knowing it.

Carlos Manuel's surrender came to fulfillment through each step of the process of his cancer treatment. But he was not deprived of the test of such total surrender many chosen souls suffered, the night of faith (*noche de fe*). Like Christ, Chali felt abandoned by the One he had planted in so many hearts throughout his apostolic life. There was no fear of death but only concern he was not prepared to die. All those around him wanted to do everything they could to help him to die as he had lived. Titay, his sister, prayed with him the service of his last Good Friday. Members of the Liturgy Circle brought him the Easter candle and sang him the Exultet, the hymn that for so many years had been part of his encounter with the risen Christ. Pepe's final attempt to help his brother was to ask him to look at the crucifix and identify with Christ's suffering. Chali's response was different: "I look but I do not find God. I am seeking the living God!" Faithful to what had been Carlos Manuel's gift in life, salvation through the resurrected, the humanized God, he died after uttering his last word: "God." His last breath came as Pepe pronounced the final words of the Exultet, "light that knows no darkness!" and knelt beside the one whom one day the Church would declare "Blessed." On July 13, 1963, the apostle of the new evangelization entered forever into full participation in Christ's resurrection. As Chali had said, indeed "The thirteenth is a good day to die!"

Thinking with the Church

Carlos Manuel lived and died for the mystery celebrated at the Easter Vigil. He was always ahead of his times. His prophetic vision was not merely his but that of the Church. His contribution to the Liturgy Circle, the Days of Christian Life, the Bulletin, and the many letters he wrote to laypeople as well as priests and sisters on the liturgical reform were all the results of his ongoing formation. He left a legacy for liturgical reform that has not yet been explored. Carlos Manuel centered all his efforts on promoting the Christian life out of the liturgical reform the Church of his times had begun. He never seemed to come across writings from a theologian or an official document of the Church that nourished him without immediately wanting to share them with others. His main legacy was that of the reform of the Easter Vigil. For Carlos Manuel, the Easter Vigil was not another Mass. *"¡No Echemos a Perder la Vigilia Pascual!"* may be one among the many articles Carlos Manuel wrote of great significance for the implementation of the Easter Vigil reform. In it, he made a strong case as to why the Easter Vigil must not be anticipated.

"The anticipation of the Easter Vigil Service at the early hours of Holy Saturday night," he wrote, "in such a way that the celebration would conclude before midnight, is something greatly improper and contrary, both to the spirit of the Service in itself, as well as the spirit of its liturgical reform carried on with such certainty and courage by our unforgettable and holy Pontiff, Pius XII, in grateful memory. Such anticipation loses all sense of the celebration. It is no longer a genuine vigil. It creates an erroneous mentality among the faithful. It frustrates those who yearn for a genuine vigil in accordance with the desire of the church. And if it is not for a grave motive, it is in complete opposition to the norms given by the Sacred Congregation of Rites" (author's translation).

The Church documents that were the sources of Carlos Manuel's liturgical ministry were also those that contributed to the theological basis for Vatican II. He studied these documents seriously as a direct call from the Church. Carlos Manuel was able to see the connection between and the importance of liturgy and the written word of God, the Bible. *Mystici Corporis*, the 1943 encyclical of Pope Pius XII, confirmed that of which Carlos Manuel already seemed convinced: a church in which all the faithful contribute to the vitality and diversity of functions, roles, and gifts. For him, this community was not one only of saints but also of sinners on the way to reconciliation with the Father through Christ. The encyclical's emphasis on the theology of the local church and the role of the bishop as teacher supported his courage to challenge liturgical leadership regarding change of rigid positions. He suffered much in trying not to have the liturgy be limited to external rubrics, which even then were in need of change. Pius XII highlighted the call of the laity to sanctity and the diversity of means to obtain it.

In the same pope's encyclical *Divino Afflante Spiritu*, also of 1943, Carlos Manuel found the necessary encouragement to his eagerness to be fed by sacred scripture. Pius XII fostered, authorized, and recognized biblical studies by the laity, a domain previously that of the clergy. Pius XII's 1947 encyclical *Mediator Dei* was the first papal document to examine and propose the basis of liturgical worship by advocating access to the faithful and giving principles to guide the celebrations. This initiative pushed the liturgical movement into a new phase as the public worship of the whole Mystical Body of Christ (head and members!). The Eucharist as the eternal salvific sacrifice of Jesus was to be the center of all Christian life. Previously Pius X had said, "The primary and indispensable source of true Christian spirit is the active participation of the assembly in the official and public prayer of the Church" (*Un Santo Puertorriqueño*, 15). Carlos Manuel not merely quoted all these references but made them the essence of his daily life.

Carlos Manuel comes across as an apostle of both the liturgical movement and the renewal of Puerto Rico (*Un Santo Puertorriqueño*, 14). The renewal of Holy Week, especially the Easter Vigil, captivated him. To this goal he gave his whole life and viewed it as the essence of the renewal. Carlos Manuel put it well when he stated: "For too long our Holy Week had remained truncated. They had replaced the Easter Climax with the Holy Sepulcher and the Pieta. . . . How much more our appreciation with the return of this triumphal song of the angels at the Easter Vigil! Alleluia! A triple celestial solemnity!" (ibid., author's translation).

Here was a layperson who realized his sense of being church and became a true apostle of the new evangelization through the heart of the life of the Church. His concern was not limited to the interior life of the Church. He was as well concerned with *inculturation* of the gospel in society even before the Church knew the word. He was constantly surprised at how little knowledge Catholics had of their faith. Through the publication of *Cultura Cristiana*, Carlos Manuel tried to bridge the gap between Christian culture and lack of knowledge on the part of the laity. Everything that he learned or read he passed on to others. He said that true leaders will have followers when they manifest certainty in what they want to hand down and enough enthusiasm about it to spread it to others. His leadership at Days of Christian Life at the Catholic University Center nurtured many committed lay Christians as well as vocations to the priesthood and religious life. As a layperson, Chali contributed to the founding of a religious community, the Sisters of Jesus Mediator, whose charism was to be a socio-religious apostolate with a Christologically centered liturgy out of which everything else would flow through the power of the Holy Spirit. Chali gave freely all that he had received. Through his work he financed his ministry.

The sanctity of the laity

Carlos Manuel's sanctity was rooted in the salvific mystery of the passion, death, and resurrection of Christ as lived and celebrated in and through the Mystical Body, the Church. For him the new evangelization was not merely focused on those who did not participate in the public worship of the Church but rather among those who worshiped not knowing fully what they celebrated. Perhaps Chali was convinced that if all Catholics understood what they celebrated, it would automatically overflow into life. Such witness would be the primary means of evangelization to those who were seeking to find the living God.

The Church continues to invite all members of the Mystical Body of Christ to become conscious of the Paschal Mystery as the center and goal of the liturgy and to participate fully in it as an endless source of grace not only for itself but for the whole world. In a special way, Carlos Manuel speaks to the laity in the Church and echoes the invitation of Christ to be perfect. Carlos Manuel's legacy to keep vigil for the coming of Christ in daily life challenges everyone to live what the Church celebrates and to celebrate genuinely what the Church claims to believe. We all have a great task of evangelization among our members, but especially that of the call to the laity as the majority in the Church to walk in the footsteps of a modern saint who took Christ's words and those of the Church seriously and lived by them. "¡Vivimos para esa noche!"

Carlos Manuel modeled the call of the U.S. Conference of Catholic Bishops in *Go and Make Disciples* by living his faith fully, sharing his faith freely, and contributing to the transformation of the world through the mystery of salvation of Christ. This legacy is his gift to the Church and to each one of us today.

References

Juan Pablo II. *Christifideles Laici: Vocación y Misión de los Laicos en la Iglesia y en el Mundo*, 1988.

¡No Echemos a Perder la Vigilia Pascual!: Carlos M. Rodríguez. Pontificia Universidad Católica de Puerto Rico: Pionet.org.

Novena al Beato Carlos M. Rodríquez Santiago. Puerto Rico: Librería Católica Anawim, 2001.

Un Santo Puertorriqueño: Carlos M. Rodríguez (1918–1963). Rio Piedras, Puerto Rico: Círculo Carlos M. Rodríguez, Centro Universitario Católico, 13 de julio de 2001.

PART III

The Liturgical Year

CHRIST COMES TO MEET US IN THE LITURGICAL YEAR: THE CHRISTMAS CYCLE

Sr. Rosa María Icaza, ccvi, PhD

T he Christmas cycle presents for our meditation the birth, infancy, adolescence, and early manhood of Jesus before he began his public life. Let us consider the Christmas cycle in its chronological order beginning with Advent, even though, as in the Easter cycle, the Lenten season developed historically after the institution of the Sacred Triduum and as a time of preparation for the climax of the liturgical year. Likewise, the Advent season as a preparation for Christmas developed several years after the Christmas feast had been assigned to December 25.

Advent

This liturgical time has two parts. The first, from the Sunday closest to November 30 to December 16, is a time of joyful expectation for the coming of Christ in Bethlehem and at the end of time. The second part is the oldest: from December 17 to 23, when the "O Antiphons" present Jesus to us (O Wisdom, December 17; O Shepherd of the House of Israel, December 18; O Shoot of Jesse's Stem, December 19; O Key of David, December 20; O Radiant Dawn, December 21; O Ruler of All Nations, December 22, and O Emmanuel, December 23). These symbols come from Hebrew scripture and describe different characteristics of Jesus; they are the Gospel acclamation verses for the respective days as well as the antiphon for the Magnificat during Evening Prayer. As do all liturgical feasts, Advent celebrates the three dimensions of time: yesterday, today, and tomorrow.

For many years, and more in some countries than others, Advent was understood to be similar to Lent: a time of preparation, penance, the use of the color purple, the presence of a *Gaudete* Sunday like the *Laetare* Sunday during Lent, and so on. Nevertheless, according to the *General Norms for the Liturgical Year and the Calendar*, Advent must be "a period for devout and joyful expectation" (no. 39). It is a joyful preparation for the arrival of a loved one; this preparation could involve some sacrifice, but sacrifice gladly made in a spirit of hope and joy.

Marian feasts

During this time of preparation, the liturgy offers us two Marian feasts: the Solemnity of the Immaculate Conception (December 8) and the Feast of Our Lady of Guadalupe (December 12). Both celebrations present Mary as helping us prepare for the coming of Jesus. When defining the dogma of the Immaculate Conception in 1854, Pope Pius IX affirmed that Mary was preserved from all sin to prepare her to be the Mother of God. Some countries, including the United States and Nicaragua, have taken Mary under this title as their patroness. Pope John Paul II also confirmed Mary under the title of Guadalupe as "Queen of All America" (*The Church in America*, no. 11). Who can better help us to prepare for Christmas than the Mother of Jesus herself?

Much could be said about the title Mary of Guadalupe: what she means for many of us; the symbols that surround her image and those that are found in the narrative of her apparitions to Saint Juan Diego and to his uncle, Juan Bernardino; the symbols we use to celebrate her feast; and so on. Let us simply mention here that the bishops of the United States have given special importance to this Marian celebration by changing the liturgical rank of December 12 from a commemoration to a feast. It is easy to combine the themes and symbols of the Guadalupe event with those of Advent, even though December 12 may be a Sunday. These two Marian feasts affirm what we read in the *Constitution on the Sacred Liturgy*:

> In celebrating this annual cycle of Christ's mysteries, the Church honors with special love Mary, the Mother of God, who is joined by an inseparable bond to the saving work of her Son. In her the Church holds up and admires the most excellent effect of the redemption and joyfully contemplates, as in a flawless image, that which the Church itself desires and hopes wholly to be (no. 103).

Christmas novena

Our popular liturgical calendar has preserved in Advent one of the customs of the first evangelization of the American continent: *Las Posadas*. It is a way to celebrate the Christmas Novena. It is based on Luke 2:1–7: Mary and Joseph had to go from Nazareth to Bethlehem where Mary "gave birth to a son, her firstborn. She wrapped him in swaddling clothes and laid him in the manger, because there was no place for them in the inn" (Luke 2:7). So, we go with Mary and Joseph on their journey and we experience, though in a limited way, the rejection and lack of hospitality when the houses where the procession goes to ask for lodging refuse (by prearrangement) to open their door, until we experience with them the happiness and security of a welcoming home. Today, in the twenty-first century, this Gospel passage should question forcefully how we receive the stranger among us. Let us remember what Jesus tells us: "Just as you did it to one of the least of these . . . you did it to me" (Matthew 25:40).

When the doors open to the pilgrims, the participants in the *Posada* enjoy friendship and joy. They enjoy special songs, games, food, and the famous piñata. An old pot or breakable vase is dressed up with cardboard and tissue paper of different colors to make it very attractive (sin always appears to us as something desirable) but in the form of a ball with seven horns (representing the seven capital sins), filled with goodies (graces from God). A child is blindfolded (a symbol of faith) and given a stick (representing fortitude) to break the pot (which is like sin that hinders us from enjoying God's graces). Some "bad" friends lead the blindfolded child the wrong way, not letting him or her break (overcome) sin. When the child finally breaks the piñata, the whole gathered community rejoices and enjoys the goodies (graces) and one another. So the whole game is a symbol of our struggle with the Evil One and of the joy of the community when Christ's friendship is recovered and there is much sharing among all those present. Likewise, when in real life we overcome sin by the grace of God, the whole community benefits from it.

On December 24, either at the end of the *Posada* or before going to Midnight Mass, many Hispanics have a simple ceremony called *La Acostada del Niño*. Because the Word of God "was made flesh" (John 1:14), born as a baby, Hispanics relate to him as truly incarnated, as one of our own. Babies need a lullaby to put them to sleep before leaving them in the crib. So, the family gathers before the Nativity scene they have prepared in a place of honor in their home. They bring out the statue of the Baby Jesus and several members of the family take turns rocking this symbol of Jesus while everyone sings Christmas carols to put him to sleep. Then, all present are invited to come and pay homage to Jesus by either touching or kissing the statue before it is placed on the manger. This simple ritual could also take place in the parish. In this case, a couple of parishioners would bring the Baby before the entrance procession that precedes Midnight Mass.

Christmas

The birth of Jesus in Bethlehem is celebrated on December 25 beginning with Midnight Mass (there is also a Vigil Mass for Christmas). The Christmas liturgy emphasizes the revelations of Jesus:

- To the poor and simple—Mary, Joseph, the shepherds—he reveals himself as human and weak.
- To the generous rich and to all those seeking Christ—the magi—he reveals himself as a special human being all of creation recognizes (star, all nations).
- To those who need his divine power and compassion—at his baptism and at the wedding of Cana—he discloses something of his divinity.

Indeed, the celebration of Epiphany, which means "manifestation," is older than that of December 25 and in the East is more solemn than Christmas night. In the West, particularly in the Northern Hemisphere and especially in Rome, some liturgical historians claim that the celebration of the birth of the sun (*natalis solis invicti*) during the winter solstice was replaced by the celebration of the birth of the Sun of Justice, Jesus. Several documents note this celebration already in the year 354 (Larson-Miller, 204–210).

The custom of having three Eucharistic celebrations for this liturgical solemnity began around the fifth and sixth centuries, particularly in Rome. First was the celebration at St. Peter's Basilica on Christmas Day with the reading of the prologue to the Gospel of John. Then a chapel was built near the Church of St. Mary where a representation of the small town of Bethlehem was honored, and so the celebration of Midnight Mass began there. The Mass at Dawn began at the Church of St. Anastasia, the center of the Byzantine presence in Rome, and as bishop of Rome the pope was also the main celebrant. In the ninth century, the emperor Charlemagne made these three celebrations the norm for Christmas in all his dominions.

During these Christmas celebrations, Jesus reveals himself to us as a poor, loved, and admired baby, but also as persecuted, migrant, and unknown. Hispanic people have taken the Incarnation of Jesus very seriously and therefore we celebrate Jesus as any other baby in our families. We decorate a special place to represent the small town of Bethlehem, or at least the place where Jesus was born. Some homes might also depict many of the major biblical stories leading to the birth of Jesus. This practice is simply called *Un Nacimiento*. Before Midnight

Sr. Rosa María Icaza, ccvi, PhD

Mass, we celebrate *La Acostada del Niño*, including the *Arrullo* (on December 24) and the "Adoration of the Baby" (on December 25). Again, this ceremony mainly happens at home. Jesus is one of us, a human baby; but Jesus is also the Son of God, so we lovingly render him homage either by kissing or touching his feet. These simple and homey ceremonies are completed when we celebrate the *Levantada del Niño* (February 2), when we commemorate that Mary and Joseph presented the Baby Jesus in the Temple (Luke 2:22–39).

From December 25 to the end of the Christmas season, there are dramatic representations of Jesus' birth called *Pastorelas*, which were another means of evangelization in the Middle Ages in Europe and in sixteenth-century America. It is easy to represent the birth of Jesus and the joy of the angels telling the shepherds to go to Bethlehem. But, as in real life, the devils also came to tempt them to stay warm and cozy instead of going in the middle of the night to look for something unexpected. Those shepherds who yielded to temptation stayed behind and missed discovering Jesus in the babe of Bethlehem. This scene may be full of laughter and mischievousness, but it teaches in a simple way what temptations can lead us to in our own lives. Our faith does not have to be serious and somber. Saint Paul wrote, "God loves a cheerful giver" (2 Corinthians 9:7).

It is interesting to see that during the Christmas Octave the liturgy also celebrates the feasts of Saint Stephen, deacon and martyr (December 26), Saint John the Evangelist (December 27), and the Holy Innocents (December 28). On this last day, many Hispanics celebrate at home by making their friends believe that something happened that did not actually happen. It is similar to what we in the United States do on April Fool's Day. Our comment when the person gets worried is, "*Inocente palomita que te dejas engañar* (Innocent little dove that is so easily deceived)." The game honors the Holy Innocents who died when Herod desired to kill Jesus whom the magi proclaimed "king."

The season continues with the celebration of Saint Thomas Becket (December 29), the Holy Family (December 30 or the Sunday within the Octave), Saint Sylvester I, pope (December 31), and on January 1, the last day of the Octave, the Solemnity of the Blessed Virgin Mary, Mother of God. With these customs, it is easier to see that we can encounter the living Christ in his followers. The saints do not take away our attention from Jesus or the Paschal Mystery, which is the core of all liturgy. On the contrary, Christ himself is revealed in the life and death of human beings, his followers, in the past, and in our time.

Epiphany

The Christmas season continues with a joyful and grateful spirit, including the great solemnity of Epiphany (January 6 or on the Sunday between January 2 and 8, which, as I stated before, dates farther back in the East than the celebration of December 25). Epiphany is the feast of the manifestation of Christ as the Son of God to all nations, not only to the Jews. There are also several cultural customs for the celebration of Epiphany that offer teachable moments for children. The magi come from the East following a star that leads them to Jesus; in real life, ideals lead us to greater things. The road to success is not easy; the magi had to ask and search. They brought symbolic gifts of gold, frankincense, and myrrh: gold to affirm Jesus' kingship, frankincense to represent his divinity, and myrrh to point out his mortal humanity. (These symbols have received other interpretations as well throughout the centuries.)

With different minor details in different countries, children learn to think of the animals the magi were riding and to leave some food and drink for them (e.g., straw and water for the camels). In gratitude, the magi leave presents for the children. Children of Mexican heritage usually clean and shine one of the shoes that took them to school every day, and in it they put straw. They place this shoe with a vessel of water on the windowsill so animals can reach it. In Puerto Rico it is the custom to put straw under the bed; in other countries people put straw in a shoebox. Whatever the children do, they learn to be mindful of and kind to animals and grateful when they benefit from a thoughtful action.

It is also customary to have a *Rosca de Reyes*, like the king cakes in New Orleans on Mardi Gras. Whoever finds the bean or the small statue of a baby in his or her piece of cake must give a party on or before the Baptism of the Lord. Once again it is a sign of joy and gratitude for finding Jesus.

On the first Sundays of Ordinary Time themes traditional to the celebration of Epiphany in the East are celebrated in the West when two other manifestations of the divinity of Jesus are recounted: the Baptism of the Lord when those present heard a voice saying, "You are my Son, the Beloved One, you are my Chosen One" and saw a dove coming to pose on Jesus' head (Luke 3:21–22); and the wedding at Cana, when Jesus changed the water into wine at his mother's request. This latter event, recorded in John's Gospel, began Jesus' "public" life.

Ordinary Time

The liturgy celebrates the words and actions of Jesus during the three years (in the Gospel of John) of his public life in the months and weeks between the great cycles of Easter and Christmas. Christ wants us to meditate on them so that we may learn how to be his true and faithful disciples.

We call these liturgical weeks "Ordinary Time" not because it is unimportant to reflect on the ways that the living Christ reveals himself and calls us to him, but because the intervening Sundays do not redound to a specific festival, are referred to by an ordinal number; hence First Sunday, Sixteenth Sunday, etc. Several liturgical feasts honor Jesus, Mary, and the saints during these weeks and months. The prayers for those days are found in the *Sanctoral,* and ask for the intercession of the saints as friends and followers of Jesus. We read in the *Constitution for the Sacred Liturgy:*

> The Church has also included in the annual cycle days devoted to the memory of the martyrs and the other saints. . . . By celebrating their passage from earth to heaven the Church proclaims the paschal mystery achieved in the saints, who have suffered and been glorified with Christ; it proposes them to the faithful as examples drawing all to the Father through Christ and pleads through their merits for God's favors (no. 104).

The list of the saints celebrated during the liturgical year has changed over the centuries. It is natural that the Church honors in a special way the apostles and martyrs who lived closer to the time of Jesus' life on earth, and then adds those saints who are closer to our times and culture. Periodically the Church simplifies the liturgical calendar, and some saints were omitted from the liturgical year during the liturgical renewal. This change allowed for the flexibility to have different celebrations within some communities such as particular dioceses, religious communities, parishes, countries, and so on (cf. *General Norms for the Liturgical Year,* nos. 49–55).

We Hispanics celebrate in a special way certain saints because we feel closer to them either because of the place where they lived and died or because they respond to our needs when we call on them to intercede for us with God. Among them: Saint Juan Diego, an indigenous man to whom Our Lady appeared at Tepeyac, Mexico; Saint Rose of Lima; Saint Martin de Porres, also from Peru, who suffered on account of his heritage—half African and half Spanish—and also because he loved and cared for poor people and animals; Saint Jude the Apostle, lovingly called *San Juditas*, because he helps in "hopeless" cases; and Saint Martin of Tours, a knight who one day upon seeing a beggar shivering with cold cut his own cape in two and gave it to him—that night Saint Martin had a dream in which he saw Jesus wearing his half-cape. Many shoemakers or carpenters have Saint Martin's picture above their main door and call on him with the prayer: "*San Martín Caballero, danos paz, salud, y dinero* (Saint Martin the Knight, grant us peace, health, and money)." His picture reminds them of Jesus' words: "Just as you did it to one of the least of these . . . you did it to me" (Matthew 25:40).

Conclusion

The liturgical year is an inexhaustible source through which Christ reveals himself to us alive in countless situations. It is said that liturgy is a constant *anamnesis* because it is not simply a remembrance, a commemoration, but it "makes present a person of the past" (cf. "Anamnesis" in *The New Dictionary of Sacramental Worship*, 45–46). The Paschal Mystery is only one; it does not repeat itself—what we repeat are the celebrations that make present to us its meaning. The liturgical year is a constant call we receive to be alert with an open heart when the living Christ comes to meet us. These encounters nourish our faith and lead us to personal conversion because we grow in our knowledge of Jesus, we love him more intensely, and he invites us to strengthen our community of brothers and sisters. Thus together we can be in solidarity with Christ suffering in the poorest and marginalized.

There is no doubt: Christ reveals himself to be alive in the liturgical year. Do we have our eyes and hearts open to receive him? If we live the liturgical year as Vatican II encourages us to—consciously, fully, and actively—we can celebrate with great joy and enthusiasm the festival that closes every liturgical year: the Solemnity of Christ the

King. We proclaim him king not only in our hearts and in our homes but also in the whole world. And like the martyrs of the religious persecution in Mexico during the 1920s, we can sing:

Que viva mi Cristo,	Long live my Christ,
que viva mi Rey,	long live my King,
Que impere doquiera	let his triumphant law
triunfante su ley.	be the rule everywhere.
¡Viva Cristo Rey! ¡Viva!	Long live Christ the King! Long Live!
¡Viva Cristo Rey!	Long live Christ the King!

References

"Anamnesis" in Peter Fink, sj, ed. *The New Dictionary of Sacramental Worship.* Collegeville, Minnesota: The Liturgical Press, 1990, 45–46.

Icaza, Rosa Maria. "When Advent Meets Guadalupe." *Preach* 1 (November–December 2003): 26–29, and in *The Treasure of Guadalupe,* Timothy Matovina and Virgilio Elizondo, eds. Notre Dame, Indiana: University of Notre Dame Press, 2006.

Larson-Miller, Lizette. "Christmas Season" in Peter Fink, sj, ed. *The New Dictionary of Sacramental Worship.* Collegeville, Minnesota: The Liturgical Press, 1990, 204–210.

CHRIST COMES TO MEET US
IN THE LITURGICAL YEAR:
THE EASTER CYCLE
Sr. Rosa María Icaza, CCVI, PhD

Our late Holy Father, John Paul II, invited us, through his apostolic exhortation *The Church in America,* "to a personal encounter with the living Christ," and he specifies the places where Jesus comes to meet us if we have eyes to see him: " 'In Sacred Scripture read in the light of Tradition . . . deepened in meditation and prayer.' In the Sacred Liturgy . . . where we are in touch with 'multiple presences of Christ' (*Constitution on the Sacred Liturgy,* no. 7) and in the poor, with whom Christ identifies himself in a particular way" (no. 12).

When Christ comes to meet us, it is always to reveal himself more deeply to each one of us and to call us to follow him more closely in the way of personal conversion, communion with our brothers and sisters, and solidarity with the poor and those excluded from our society.

The liturgical year invites us to celebrate with gratitude and reverence the birth, life, passion, death, and resurrection of Our Lord Jesus Christ and to enter into the spirit of each liturgical season with conviction and enthusiasm as true followers of Christ. "The celebration of the different feasts in the liturgical year is a concrete and pedagogical way to celebrate the Paschal Mystery that we must live every day of our lives" (Jean Lebon, *How to Understand the Liturgy,* New York, Crossroad, 1986, 89).

The liturgical year is divided into two major cycles: the Easter cycle and the Christmas cycle, with several intervening Sundays simply named in succession by numbers: First, Second, Third, and so on Sundays in Ordinary Time. In fact, immediately at the end of the Christmas cycle (from Advent to the Feast of the Baptism of the Lord, which is also the First Sunday in Ordinary Time) we begin with the Second Sunday in Ordinary Time; then, the numbering of the Sundays is interrupted to celebrate the Easter cycle (from Ash Wednesday to Pentecost Sunday), but the numbering resumes at the beginning of the following Advent season. "Ordinary Time" is not a name implying mundane, unimportant Sundays, but is a name derived from using *ordinal* numbers (first, second, and so on).

To commemorate the life, passion, death, and resurrection of Christ liturgically means not only to bring back to mind (to remember) but also to bring back to the heart (*recordar: cor*=heart), which means to feel what Jesus did and suffered for our salvation. In each celebration Christ comes to encounter us, offering special graces and strength to follow him and be his faithful disciples. We read in the *Catechism of the Catholic Church*:

> Christian liturgy not only recalls the events that saved us but actualizes them, makes them present. The Paschal Mystery of Christ is celebrated, not repeated. It is the celebrations that are repeated, and in each celebration there is an outpouring of the Holy Spirit that makes the unique mystery present (no. 1104).

Christ makes himself present in "the person of His minister [who presides] . . . in the Eucharistic species . . . in the sacraments . . . in His word . . . in the gathered assembly. In the liturgy, the sanctification of man [*sic*] is manifested by signs perceptible to the senses, and is effected in a way which is proper to each of these signs" (*Constitution on the Sacred Liturgy*, no. 7). The living Christ comes to encounter each of us. Do we have our eyes open to see him? Are our hearts ready to receive him? If we are aware of this encounter, we cannot help but go out to share it with our brothers and sisters through our words and example.

Sunday: The Lord's Day

The original liturgical celebration in the Church is Sunday. It is a weekly Easter. Each Gospel writer manifests insistently that the risen Jesus reveals himself to the church, the gathered assembly, on the first day of the week. This fact shows plainly the importance of that day. It is the day on which we gather to carry out what Jesus asked of us: to "do this in memory of me" (Luke 22:19; 1 Corinthians 11:23–25). The first Christians valued this encounter with Christ during the Sunday celebration as something so important that they were willing to give their lives, and they considered the Sunday celebration an essential part of being a Christian: "I devoutly celebrated the mysteries of the Lord, and I gathered with my brothers and sisters, because I am a Christian" (cf. D. Ruiz Bueno, *Actas de los Mártires,* BAC 75, 975–994).

The liturgy continually calls us to repentance, to conversion, to live a new and different lifestyle. As I already stated, the heart of the liturgy is the Paschal Mystery: the mystery of God's initiative and our response as it reveals God's self in the life, passion, death, and resurrection of the Lord. Liturgical renewal endeavors to focus more clearly on the Paschal Mystery of Christ as the core of all liturgical acts. This fact, however, does not mean we should omit celebrations in honor of the saints, because by their lives and example they show us Christ living in them and how we can also follow in the footsteps of the Lord.

The liturgical year is the structure within which we celebrate the different aspects of the mystery of the life, passion, death, and resurrection of Christ. The key to this structure is Sunday, the Lord's Day. How much time do we give on that day to be with God? Do we go to Mass because it is an obligation—because we have always done so? Because we desire to be *with* our Friend we desire to worship God, to give thanks, to ask for help, and to ask pardon not only for ourselves but also for our brothers and sisters? Do we go with enthusiasm each Sunday to *meet with the living Christ*?

The Sacred Triduum

From this Sunday experience the Sacred Triduum began to celebrate with greater detail and intensity the key moments of the last days of the life, passion, death, and resurrection of Jesus. Initially the Sacred Triduum was celebrated beginning on Thursday at sundown and lasted until sundown on Sunday. Later in the history of Lent and the Triduum the holiest days of the year came to be Thursday, Friday, and Saturday. After 1955 the Sacred Triduum was restored to the original way of counting the days: It begins on Thursday at sundown or the celebration of the Mass of the Lord's Supper and ends with the second vespers of Easter Sunday.

During the Sacred Triduum we, particularly Hispanics, practice one of our cultural values: to accompany, to be with those who suffer (crying with those who cry, consoling the afflicted as a work of mercy), and we try to be near Jesus almost constantly.

Holy Thursday

On Holy Thursday, besides participating in the liturgical ceremonies—Mass, procession, and adoration of the Blessed Sacrament—we take a small loaf of blessed bread to our homes to share with those who due to illness or other reasons are not able to go to church and participate in the celebration. We meet the living

Christ when we participate in the Eucharist, and we desire that our brothers and sisters also meet him even though it is in a symbolic way: "breaking bread" together.

We also have the custom of the "candle of the Blessed Sacrament," which is lit at the altar of repose after the liturgical services on Holy Thursday. Then the candle is taken home to light before and during a storm. Its light will remind us that Jesus, the Light of the world, is in our midst, but it also serves a practical purpose: When a storm knocks out the electricity, the lit candle shines in the darkness just as Jesus always accompanies us—and with greater tenderness during difficult moments. The sacred and the practical, the symbolic and the real are one.

But that night we cannot go to our homes to rest; we continue living the liturgy, because we have the custom of going to one or more churches or altars of repose to spend a few moments with Jesus in the Eucharist. Even though it is not well known in the United States and not much practiced today, this tradition includes a visit to seven churches to accompany Jesus as he was taken to seven different places that night after the Last Supper. During those visits, we usually pray in private, but the whole family goes together. We begin at the Garden of Olives, meditating on Jesus' agony and Judas' treason.

We remember (during the first visit) how Jesus was taken prisoner and dragged before Annas, who had been a high priest and still had great influence over his son-in-law, Caiaphas, the current high priest (John 18:12–23). There Jesus was questioned about his disciples and his teachings; it was the place where a soldier hit Jesus in the face, and Jesus defended himself by saying, "If I have spoken wrongly, point it out; but if I have spoken rightly, why do you strike me?" (John 18:23). Here we may think of all those who have suffered an undeserved punishment. They also reveal to us the living Jesus. How do we judge them? Do we dare impose the death penalty?

Thus we can continue meeting and being with Jesus as he is taken from one place to another. We see Jesus at:

• Caiaphas' house (second visit), when "Annas sent him, bound, to Caiaphas, the High Priest" (John 18:24). There "they tried to find some evidence against Jesus so that they might put him to death" (Mark 14:53, 55).

• The Sanhedrin (third visit), where "the chief priests and the whole Supreme Council needed some false evidence against Jesus, so that they might put him to death" (Matthew 26:59–67; Luke 22:66–71).

They mocked Jesus but were unable to condemn him because it was night. During those moments Jesus reveals himself to us as someone his disciples abandoned and Peter denied (Luke 22:54–62).

• The Roman governor's court (fourth visit): Jesus reveals himself to us as dignified and secure in himself although when it was morning the members of the Supreme Council condemned him as a blasphemer because Jesus affirmed his identity. Then they took him to Pilate (Luke 23:1–5; John 18:28–40), accusing him of being a revolutionary.

• Herod's court (fifth visit): At that time, "Herod happened to be in Jerusalem," so Pilate, upon hearing that Jesus was a Galilean and therefore under Herod's jurisdiction, sent Jesus to the tetrarch to be judged (Luke 23:6–14), but Herod simply ridiculed Jesus and sent him back to Pilate.

• Pilate's court (sixth visit): The Roman governor again tried to avoid condemning Jesus to death, but humiliated him by scourging him (Luke 23:13–25). What was Jesus feeling when the chief priests and the crowd shouted, "Crucify him! Crucify him!" (John 19:6)? What do our brothers and sisters feel when we ignore them?

• Mount Calvary (seventh visit): Pilate finally handed Jesus over to those who were asking for his crucifixion and sent him to Calvary to be crucified (John 19:1–16). We meditate on Jesus' suffering in his body and in his spirit on seeing himself condemned because he had affirmed the truth: his own identity as the Son of God and God's unconditional love for each of us.

Good Friday

After this meditation, we relive the way of the cross on Good Friday as we participate in the liturgy of this day: the Liturgy of the Word with the proclamation of the Passion and the Solemn Prayers, the veneration of the cross, and the reception of Holy Communion. Although not liturgically permitted, in some parishes people dramatize the reading of the Passion through the neighborhood streets so that many people actively participate and accompany Jesus during the last hours before his death. In the United States, San Antonio hosts perhaps the best known example. All of this helps us to meet the living Christ who shows us his great love for us. What is our response when we see those who suffer because of violence or who are victims of injustice and of hatred?

Furthermore, besides participating in the liturgy of Good Friday, we Hispanics have three other beautiful customs: "The Seven Words," "Procession to the Place of Burial," and "Condolences to Mary." We feel the need to live the liturgy as we celebrate it with our loved ones. When someone dies, we consider their last wishes as something very sacred. Over and over again we repeat the words we heard and try to make them a reality. This is what we do when we meditate on the words that Jesus said the seven times he spoke at Calvary. All of them come from the Gospels:

1. "Father, forgive them for they do not know what they do" (Luke 23:34).
2. "God, my God, why have you forsaken me?" (Matthew 27:46; Mark 15:34).
3. "Truly, you will be with me today in paradise" (Luke 23:43).
4. "Woman, this is your son . . . . There is your mother" (John 19:26–27).
5. "I am thirsty" (John 19:28).
6. "It is accomplished" (John 19:30).
7. "Father, into your hands, I commend my spirit" (Luke 23:46).

What do these words mean for me? Have I cried similar words in my life? Have I heard some of my brothers or sisters say them? How do I respond?

When a person mourns the death of a loved one, we cannot leave him or her alone. For this reason, we continue living our liturgy by participating in the burial procession and in offering our *Pésame*—our Condolence—to Jesus' mother, Mary. As we have just mentioned, Jesus told us, in the person of the apostle John, "There is your mother" (John 19:27). The Gospel continues: "And from that moment the disciple took her to his own home." Have we received Mary as our mother? Is Mary at home with us? There is a beautiful and simple hymn in Spanish that says: "As you go through life, you are never alone, / On the way, Holy Mary goes with you." Do we believe that? How do we relate personally to Mary?

Frequently we go to Mary asking her to intercede for us as she did at the wedding feast at Cana (John 2:3). On this day, Good Friday, when we commemorate the death of her Son, Jesus, could we leave her alone? There is no particular ceremony, prayer, or hymn the Church prescribes for this celebration. The main point is that we, as an assembly and members of a parish, want to express our condolences not only to Mary but to all our brothers and sisters who feel alone and abandoned because one of their loved ones has died. The living Christ reveals himself to us in them and through them as we offer our condolences to Mary.

Holy Saturday

Holy Saturday, which before the renewal of Vatican II used to be called in Spanish *Sábado de Gloria*, is one of the liturgical days that has changed more in the way we celebrate it. Now it should be a day of intense preparation for the Easter Vigil, and we are encouraged to fast in support of the catechumens and candidates who are preparing to become full members of the Catholic Church.

It feels like an empty day after the intensity of the celebrations of Holy Thursday and Good Friday. Jesus is lying in the tomb, and the Church does not gather for any celebration until the great Easter Vigil. We feel deeply the physical presence of Jesus and with greater longing we wait for his resurrection.

The liturgical celebration of the Easter Vigil includes many concrete symbols: fire, light, the Easter candle, holy water, bells, flowers, and others—everything that symbolizes new life. This liturgy is the climax of the entire liturgical year. Heaven and earth rejoice with Jesus' triumph and with the new members of the body of Christ who receive the sacraments of initiation. The joyful alleluias resound with gratitude and strength. It is indeed a "holy night."

Easter Sunday

The liturgical celebration continues through the whole Sunday, the main Sunday of the whole liturgical year: Easter Sunday. In some countries, like the Philippines, there is a beautiful custom early on this day. It is an expression of the special place that Mary has among Hispanic peoples and of how faith is incarnated in our human life. The custom is *La procession del santo encuentro*—the procession to the holy encounter between the risen Jesus and his mother Mary. The Bible does not mention anything about this event, but the people think it is common sense that Jesus, who had a loving relationship with Mary, his mother, would appear first to her after his resurrection.

Usually, the procession, carrying a statue of Mary, begins from a church on the west side of the town, and at the same time another procession carrying a statue of the risen Jesus begins from a church on the east side. They meet in front of the cathedral or at the center of town.

_____ *Sr. Rosa María Icaza, ccvi, PhD*

Song, music, and joyful expressions accompany all this movement. In other countries, like El Salvador, other statues of different saints come out also in procession from other churches to meet and congratulate Jesus. Heaven and earth are rejoicing with Jesus in his day of triumph over death!

In other cultures, the Easter celebration includes other customs, like freshly baked bread; blessed water (named in Spanish *agua florida*); decorated eggs (because a chick comes out of a shell as Jesus did from the tomb); the Easter bunny (an animal that reproduces itself abundantly, symbolizing the abundant life Jesus gives us, cf. John 10:10: "I came that you may have life and life in abundance"); *cascarones* (eggshells filled with confetti that symbolize God's graces as people break the shells on the head of friends); flowers (that bloom at the beginning of spring), which give the name to this Sunday in Spanish: *La Pascua Florida* (in 1513, Juan Ponce de León discovered the peninsula on Easter Sunday, hence its name—Florida); and others. All these customs are symbols of life, of joy, because "we live in our daily life what we have celebrated in the liturgy." The encounter with the living Christ in the liturgical celebrations gives meaning and depth to our daily living. We should also note that the Northern Hemisphere has given these celebrations a greater importance than the Southern Hemisphere, where during the civic year the seasons of the year are reversed.

Indeed, particularly after the liturgical renewal, the Church does not celebrate only on one Sunday but continues through the next fifty days ending with the Solemnity of Pentecost. From the early centuries, the church has celebrated these days with the neophytes, those newly baptized, who receive more instruction in the faith in order to fulfill the mission that Jesus gave us: "Go and make disciples from all nations [helping them to know, to personally encounter, Jesus]. Baptize them in the Name of the Father and of the Son and of the Holy Spirit [celebrating the sacraments of initiation at the Easter Vigil], and teach them to fulfill all I have commanded you [instructing them in the truths of faith during the Easter season]" (Matthew 28:19–20a). That period is what today we call *mystagogia,* that is, to know more deeply the symbols and meaning of the initiation sacraments, the mystery of the saving life, death, and resurrection of Jesus, and to affirm our encounter with Christ through our living out his teachings. That is true evangelization: personal encounter with the living Christ, celebration of the sacraments, catechesis to know how to fulfill God's will.

Lent

Later in the history of the Church, the initial simple time of preparation for the Sacred Triduum (a solemn fast of forty hours) was extended, first to a forty-day period and then to a period of forty fast days (which is why we begin Lent on Ash Wednesday: to have forty fast days, because Sundays are never fast days). This forty fast-day period is Lent. It is time of purification (conversion) and prayer. Let us continue our reflection on the liturgical year by looking back to this Lenten season, which initiates for us the Easter season.

Lent begins on Ash Wednesday and ends at sundown on Holy Thursday or with the celebration of the Lord's Supper on Holy Thursday. During this time the Church recommends the practices of fasting, prayer, and almsgiving (good works or works of mercy; giving of time, talent, and treasure). We also have cultural customs among parish communities and as a Christian people—for example, parish missions and the Way of the Cross. Lent, as all of our celebrations, includes spiritual and human elements. There are certain typical dishes for Lent: lentil soup, *nopalitos*, shrimp croquettes, *capirotada*. Every thing happens to help us prepare for the celebration of Easter in time and in eternity.

During this time of Lenten preparation, we encounter the living Christ particularly in the Gospels of each Sunday. The First Sunday of Lent includes the proclamation of the Gospel that speaks of the temptations of Jesus in the desert (Year A: Matthew 4:1–11; Year B: Mark 1:12–15; Year C: Luke 4:1–13). We see him praying and fasting; then, we are witnesses to how he overcomes three temptations. *Jesus is very human*, as anyone of us knows who needs prayer and penance to overcome the things that attract us but draw us away from God. During the Second Sunday, Christ is revealed in his transfiguration to help us not to lose sight of his *divinity*.

The other Lenten Sundays present to us a Jesus filled with compassion and mercy, instructing the Samaritan woman, curing the man who was blind from birth, and resuscitating Lazarus during Year A; reclaiming the Temple as the house of God, announcing his death on the cross to save us, and emphasizing with the parable of the grain of wheat that if we look for life we must pass through death, during Year B; and seeking our conversion, as in the story of the fig tree, giving us the beautiful example of the parable of the prodigal son, and his generous pardon of the woman caught in adultery, during Year C.

How many lessons and examples does Jesus give us to tell us that, with his grace, we will encounter him alive in our brothers and sisters! We must always ask ourselves at the different moments in our life: What would Jesus do in this situation? What would Jesus say? We must live what we have celebrated in the liturgy because at the end of each Eucharistic liturgy, we are sent to proclaim the Good News.

We usually call the Sixth Sunday of Lent "Palm Sunday." On this Sunday we reflect on the Passion of Christ. It is the immediate preparation for the Sacred Triduum, and it is a source of meditation on the infinite love of Jesus for each one of us. If we are aware of Christ's presence in our liturgical celebrations, we cannot but follow his example in our daily living. Thus we see how this long preparation helps us to celebrate with greater depth the great mystery of salvation and to know more closely our Lord and Savior.

Conclusion

Although the chronological order of the Easter cycle is Lent (from Ash Wednesday to Holy Thursday evening), the Sacred Triduum (from Thursday evening to Easter Sunday evening), and the Easter season (the following fifty days ending with Pentecost Sunday), we have reflected on it in the order of its importance within the liturgical year.

It has become easier to understand the importance of Sunday, which is an abbreviated celebration of the mystery of God's love revealed in the passion, death, and resurrection of our Lord and Savior. It helps to see our own life in the light of Jesus' passion, death, and resurrection and to see God's tender mercy in the midst of struggles and concerns. Suffering and death are very real, but they are not the end; we confidently wait for eternal life.

The official liturgical celebrations of the Church together with some of the Hispanic community's cultural expressions of faith are truly vehicles and symbols that help each one of us enter more deeply into the mysteries of life and participate more actively and meaningfully in the weekly and annual celebrations of the mystery of salvation. We can truly experience encounters with the living Jesus Christ in liturgical celebrations and in our daily living of conversion, communion, and solidarity.

PART IV

Music

LITURGY TO LIVE—
LIVE FOR THE LITURGY
Most Rev. Ricardo Ramírez, CSB

A few weeks before my Grandmother "Panchita" had her final encounter with the Lord, I had been appointed auxiliary bishop of San Antonio. Before a celebration I asked my grandmother—who was 90 at the time—what she liked to do for fun. She said she went to funerals. I asked her, "How can you have fun at a funeral?" and she answered, "Son, haven't you learned yet that it is a privilege to die?" Indeed, throughout all my studies I had never thought about death in these terms.

When I saw her for the last time, she told me, "I want to see the Lord's face! I only want to see the Lord's face!" My aunts tell me that as she was dying she would sing songs from her childhood, "*Al cielo, al cielo quiero ir.*" Yes, thanks to my Grandmother Panchita, I learned that for Christians, death is a privilege, because it is the encounter for which we came to this world, so that some day we can meet the Lord and see his face.

There is no doubt that an encounter with the living Christ refers to the encounter that occurs and that we feel during the liturgy. It is also the encounter we celebrate each time we "eat this bread and drink this cup."

The encounter

We can encounter Christ in many different ways. I will try to relate some of these encounters to the liturgy and especially to the ministry of sacred music.

We find him in creation. We encounter God when we see every creature, big and small, for creation is a reflection of God. Artists, through their creative intuition, capture the divinity we feel in creation. There are also sounds: the water from a small river that is carried over stones or a tall waterfall that thunders as it comes down, or the waves as they break on the shore; in the sounds of birds, dogs, cats, cows, chickens, whales, wind, thunder, and rain. God is revealed through these sounds and noises. "The heavens declare the glory of God, and the firmament proclaims his handiwork . . . . through all the earth their voice resounds, and to the ends of the world, their message. He has pitched a tent there for the sun" (Psalm 19:1–5). Musicians imitate the melody of nature, its rhythms, its highs and lows, the loudness and softness of its melodies. Members of the *cursillos* capture the spirit to which I am referring in the Spanish song that says,

> *Canta el gallo, canta el gallo con el quiri-quiri-quiri-quiri-quiri.*
> *La gallina, la gallina con el cara-cara-cara-cara-cara.*
> *Los polluelos, los polluelos con el pío-pío-pío-pi.*
> *Y por eso los grandes amores de muchos colores me gustan a mí.*
> *Y por eso los grandes amores de muchos colores me gustan a mí.*

Music discovers and captures the music already present in creation. And when musicians compose music and sing it in the liturgy, they attempt to create an encounter between God and the faithful. Theirs is an awesome responsibility.

The greatest encounter is with God-made-flesh. It is the Word that comes to "live among us." This phrase is an allusion to the Hebrew *skene-sekinah*, meaning "tabernacle or meeting tent" (Exodus 33:7), which is normally translated as "the word made flesh." In reality the temple is for us the "meeting tent" where we encounter the Word-made-flesh, the living Christ. When Jesus Christ became man, we saw the perfect union between God and man. Jesus Christ is God and man at the same time, not divided; there exists a perfect union of both natures, God and man are united in one person. For this reason Mary is the Mother of God, because Mary is the Mother of the God-Man, who is one person.

We could say that the first liturgy took place when the Word became flesh in Mary's womb. An encounter also takes place there, and Mary responds with the Magnificat. Mary is the first music minister; she is the first one to worship the God-man in the name of all those who would become members of the people of God.

For me one of the most dramatic moments of God's encounter with humankind is Christ on the cross. Suspended between heaven and earth, he unites humanity with God. The vertical part of the cross reminds us that God comes to us through God's Son Jesus. The horizontal part of the cross reminds us of ourselves, fallen because of our sins, but raised by all that transcends material and earthly things.

An encounter happens when two people meet. Many times a third person introduces two people. In Christ we encounter God the Father. He is the "sacrament of the encounter with God." A sacrament is something living and dynamic. It means what it does and it does what it means.

A sacrament means and makes present another reality. Jesus Christ is the "personal sacrament" of the Father—Christ, who says, "Whoever sees me, sees my Father, whoever hears me, hears my Father." At the same time, the liturgy's main function is to announce Christ. The divine sacrifice of the Eucharist is the outstanding means whereby the faithful may express in their lives, and manifest to others, the mystery of Christ (*Constitution on the Sacred Liturgy*, no. 2). "Each time we eat this bread and we drink this blood, we announce your death, Lord, until you return."

Just as catechists or evangelizers have the duty to introduce God to others, and make the encounter with Christ possible, ministers of sacred music have the privilege and the duty to introduce the living Christ to the faithful. Their responsibility is to introduce God to the people and the people to God. In this task they perform the same duty as the presider, the priest.

In the liturgy, music ministers also perform and make palpable the priesthood of the faithful, the one they received in baptism. It is up to them to unite others during the liturgy with Christ, the head of the mystical body. "God of kings, holy people, priestly people, people of God, bless your Lord." During the liturgy we all participate in the eternal priesthood of our Lord Jesus Christ.

Music ministers also help the faithful recognize and discover Christ among them. "When two or three are gathered in my name, I am there also." Through this unique sacred encounter we receive the gift of life. "I have come so that you can have life and have it abundantly." We also recall that he is "the way, the truth, and the life."

We must not forget that encounter is a pathway to communion. When I receive the consecrated bread, I say, "*Amen!* I believe that I am about to unite with Christ by way of this sacred food. *Amen!* I believe that I am also united with the Father and with the Holy Spirit, because the Son is never separated from the other Persons of the Holy Trinity. *Amen!* I believe that Christ is in the person in front of me, behind me, at my right, and at my left." At the same time we unite with those who have died in the faith and who enjoy glory in heaven. I am referring to the communion of the saints; I also unite with those saints who have yet to be born (cf. *Catechism of the Catholic Church*, no. 949ff). It is a moment that transcends the present. "In the liturgy we experience Christ today, Christ yesterday, and Christ forever."

Ritual and the liturgy

A rite is a ceremonial act, guided by rules, that people organize and when carried out puts them in communion with the divine. Rites are practiced in order to praise God, to ask for favors and for forgiveness, or give thanks. At times rites have included sacrifices aimed to please a god or gods.

For us Christians, rites are everything that we do at prayer, during the liturgy or in popular religiosity. Every Hispanic community has its own rites, by which they are identified and by which they relate with God, Mary, and all the saints. At the same time in their popular rituals there is an intuition or feeling that unites them with their ancestors or with those who will come. Thus popular religiosity is an expression of the communion of saints.

Popular religiosity continues to be one of the main ways by which our people hand on their faith from generation to generation. For this reason it is of utmost importance to keep the music that keeps these rites alive for the people. Is it possible that we may be forgetting some of the most popular songs to Mary?

Spirituality and the music minister

Liturgical spirituality is not something apart from everything else. Liturgy must connect us with life, and what we do in life we should take to the liturgy. The liturgy and our daily lives must nurture one another. Our Lord called us to "worship the Father in Spirit and truth" (John 4:23). This means that our prayers and worship should be truthful, and our lives should reflect that truthfulness.

The need to unite the liturgy with our lives challenges all of us, but liturgical ministers must pay special attention to the challenge of developing a better and more honest liturgical spirituality.

Prayer and contemplation must inspire our lives. We cannot gather around the altar with our hands empty. They must be full of faith and the love of God, and this will only happen when one has a well-established faith life. Because spirituality is connected with daily life, we are aware that how we live as disciples is connected directly with our celebration of the Mass.

Music leaders, cantors, and music ministers have the serious obligation to develop their liturgical spirituality. I used to think that in classical music the good musicians were those who played or sang the right notes. It was not until later that I found out that the good musicians were those who put their life and soul into the music they interpreted. If those who play classical or secular music should be very concerned about the spirit of these kinds of music, how much more concerned should those who play religious music be?

Practical suggestions

1. This first suggestion is the most important one. It has to do with appreciating and recognizing the intent of the composer. Let us remember that many of the texts of the songs we sing during the liturgy sometimes come from strong human and Christian experiences. Think of the popular song *Pescador de Hombres (Lord, You Have Come)* by Cesáreo Gabaráin:

> *Tú has venido a la orilla,*
> *No has buscado ni a sabios ni a ricos;*
> *Tan sólo quieres que yo te siga.*

> *Señor, me has mirado a los ojos,*
> *Sonriendo has dicho mi nombre,*
> *En la arena he dejado mi barca,*
> *Junto a ti buscaré otro mar.*

> Lord, you have come to the seashore,
> Neither searching for the rich nor the wise,
> Desiring only that I should follow.

> O Lord, with your eyes set upon me,
> gently smiling you have spoken my name,
> All I longed for I have found by the water;
> At your side, I will seek other shores.

Look at the text from a song written by Juan Antonio Espinosa:

> *Desterrados, muy lejos de esa tierra*
> *Que hace tiempo nos vio por vez primera;*
> *Junto al fuego de unos cuantos palos secos,*
> *En la noche cantamos nuestras penas.*

> Uprooted, far from that land
> That long ago saw us first,
> By the fire of a few dry logs,
> At night we sing our sorrows.

These songs certainly came from very profound experiences of Christian life. We must imagine we are having a conversation with the songwriter.

"What is your message?"

The songwriter answers, "Examine the text I composed or that I chose from sacred scripture. Let your singing style reflect my message. Also remember that there is an intimate connection between the text and the music. The music gives life to the text. The music is at the service of the text."

In interviews with various sacred and secular musicians, I learned some interesting things about music ministry. My question to them was, "What message could I give to Hispanic pastoral musicians?" One member of a trio that plays Mexican music said that when he was a seminarian his music teacher would always insist, "Concentrate on the words!" That same piece of advice has helped him even as he sings secular music. Mary Frances Reza told me that the "text has power," especially when it comes from the Bible. The text evangelizes, converts, and transmits the grace of forgiveness, of love, and of peace.

2. Sing with gusto! Don't forget that your music has a deep impact on the hearts of those who listen to it. Salvador Hernández, a mariachi music singer in Las Cruces, told me that when he sings he wants "*¡que la gente se sienta bonito!* (for people to feel good inside)."

Carlos Corral, one of my colleagues in the Diocese of Las Cruces, shared with me that he was raised in a small town called El Ojito in Chihuahua. When the family left Chihuahua to seek a better life in the United States, Carlos was a young boy. His Catholic faith had come to him especially through his grandmother's influence back in Chihuahua, and when the family left, he thought they were leaving God behind. He was sad that God would not be with him in this new land.

Then his mother took him to a church in New Mexico, and he heard a hymn to the Blessed Virgin that he had heard back home. From then on he breathed easier, for God was in the United States, too! His son, Andrés, when he was young, asked his father while they were driving home from church, "Dad, what does 'the Lord is kind and merciful' mean?" The repetition of the psalm's response remains in the minds of children. Salvador Hernández, to whom I referred earlier, says that his three-year-old daughter gets distracted during Mass and starts to play. When it is time to sing the Our Father, however, that little girl wakes up, gets on her feet, puts her little hands together, and sings the Our Father together with the rest of the congregation. She does this every time they attend Mass.

Music in the liturgy has to come from within, from the heart, the soul, for music is a gift from God, and it is the language of the heart. As Salvador said, music expresses our feelings. Mary Frances shared something from Arturo Campos, a New Mexico historian, who said, "The song is the most lyrical and most subjective manifestation of the soul of any culture, and through its music, we can hear the rhythm of its people."

3. Rehearsal is important. Because music ministry is so important in order to give life to the liturgy, musicians need to work hard to make the music sound its best during the liturgy. For this reason rehearsals are not only important and useful but absolutely necessary. Liturgical musicians need to be well prepared and to take rehearsal time seriously. Musical improvisation during the liturgy is unacceptable.

4. Be creative, but don't take on the role of performer. Invite others in the congregation to sing along. Don't forget that your role is not to entertain. The people's attention should be geared toward what is going on at the altar, not toward those who play and sing the music. In addition, it is possible to include an area's culture in moments of musical creativity.

5. Include new people, especially young people, in the choir. Choirs can sometimes become exclusive, and it becomes difficult for new people to become part of them. It is important to include young people, for we older people will some day have to leave the music ministry, and someone will have to take our places.

6. Take some time right before the Mass to rehearse with the assembly. This rehearsal is of utmost importance, especially when introducing a new song. It is also good to rehearse the responsorial psalm. The more I experience the liturgy, the more I see the importance of the psalm. There is no other song that has such potential to penetrate the hearts and to contribute to the contemplative aspects of the liturgy. One year we had three ordinations at our cathedral in Las Cruces. It was an unforgettable ceremony, and when I asked people how they liked the ordination, their eyes filled up with tears, they were so overwhelmed with emotion. And when I asked them what part they liked best, they said, "When we sang the responsorial psalm." The reason was because the cantor sang with all her heart, "*Qué alegría cuando me dijeron 'vamos a la casa del Señor, vamos a la casa del Señor'* (I rejoiced when I heard them say, 'Let us go to the house of the Lord, let us go to the house of the Lord')."

7. Don't forget the children. First, we must not lose sight of the simple songs we learned from our grandparents. How can we transmit from one generation to the next the secular songs from Pedro Infante, Lola Beltrán, Agustín Lara, and José Alfredo Jiménez? We can and should also teach sacred music to future generations. I don't think we are taking advantage of music in our religious education programs. Through music we can teach catechism. We should challenge songwriters to write new music for children.

8. Sing appropriate songs for specific moments of the Mass: the procession, the presentation of the gifts, the acclamations, Communion, meditation, and exit song.

9. Be aware of your behavior during Mass. This awareness was not as necessary before because the choir had its own place, the choir loft; the choir was heard, not seen. Now the choir tends to be in front, where the entire assembly can see them. Be aware of your behavior—not reading your music, for example, during the readings or during the homily. Always maintain an attitude of piety and reverential attention, and in this way you will be a good example for others.

10. Pay close attention to your prayer life. For all of us who lead the faithful in the official prayer of the Church, it is important that we maintain a personal and communal prayer life. We can all pay more attention to prayers. None of us is happy with the amount of time or the quality of our prayers. It is true that the more we pray, the more we want to pray, and the less we pray, the less we want to pray. In this context, I recommend retreats and also retreats with choirs from other Masses and parishes. As well as praying together, these retreats can take advantage of the opportunity to sing together and enrich one other.

Conclusion

We are grateful to musicians for what they do to bring their best musical gifts to the Lord's throne. They help us worship and glorify our God. I would like to repeat the words of "The Little Drummer Boy," the song about the little boy who did not have gold, myrrh, or incense to give to the newborn child in Bethlehem. He only had the "pa rum pum pum pum" of his drum.

> *El camino que lleva a Belén*
> *baja hasta el valle que la nieve cubrió.*
> *Los pastorcillos quieren ver a su Rey,*

le traen regalos en su humilde zurrón
al Redentor, al Redentor.

Yo quisiera poner a tus pies
algún presente que te agrade Señor,
mas Tú ya sabes que soy pobre también,
y no poseo más que un viejo tambor.

(rom pom pom pom, rom pom pom pom)

¡En tu honor frente al portal tocaré con mi tambor!

El camino que lleva a Belén
voy marcando con mi viejo tambor,
nada hay mejor que yo pueda ofrecer,
su ronco acento es un canto de amor
al Redentor, al Redentor.

Cuando Dios me vio tocando ante Él, me sonrió.

Come they told me, *pa rum pum pum pum.*
A new born king to see, *pa rum pum pum pum.*

Our finest gifts we bring, *pa rum pum pum pum.*
To lay before the king, *pa rum pum pum pum,*
rum pum pum pum, rum pum pum pum.
So to honor him, *pa rum pum pum pum,*
When we come.

Little baby, *pa rum pum pum pum.*
I am a poor boy, too, *pa rum pum pum pum.*
I have no gift to bring, *pa rum pum pum pum.*
That's fit to give a king, *pa rum pum pum pum,*
rum pum pum pum, rum pum pum pum.
Shall I play for you, *pa rum pum pum pum,*
On my drum.

Mary nodded, *pa rum pum pum pum.*
The ox and lamb kept time, *pa rum pum pum pum.*
I played my drum for him, *pa rum pum pum pum.*
I played my best for him, *pa rum pum pum pum,*
rum pum pum pum, rum pum pum pum.

Then he smiled at me, *pa rum pum pum pum,*
Me and my drum.

LITURGICAL MUSIC IN HISPANIC CATHOLIC ASSEMBLIES OF THE U.S.

Father Juan J. Sosa

Though not a professional or an academic musician, music—and specifically liturgical music—has become both an inspiration for my pastoral work and the expression of my spiritual journey. I would like to divide my reflections into three parts; then, I hope to offer a few personal conclusions on this topic. The three major sections of my reflections will include the following: first, "music as symbol and prayer;" second, "Hispanic liturgy in the United States;" and third, "Spanish liturgical music in Hispanic worship."

Music as symbol and prayer

Social scientists have assisted bishops and pastors, theologians, liturgists, musicians, and, in general, all pastoral agents of the church to understand the nature and function of symbols in individuals and cultural groups. Religious symbols, either *dominant* or *instrumental*, as constitutive of the ritual system of each cultural group, define the group itself, which, through its symbols, reveals its values, its priorities, and even the intricacies of its individual members' relationships to God and one another. Religious symbols, like other symbols, function in specific ways. As distinct from signs, symbols first evoke in the members of the group the deeper reality they represent, and second, involve them with the depth of that reality and the impact "it" brings about.

Having heard many eloquent reflections on one of today's most popular terms in Church circles, *inculturation*, I cannot help but recall a brief but wonderful article written by Father Theodore Zuern, sj, and published in 1983 by the Centre "Cultures and Religions" of the Pontifical Gregorian University. Titled "The Preservation of Native Identity in the Process of Inculturation, as Experienced in American Indian Cultures," the article provides a set of valuable ideas from which all pastoral agents can profit, whether their pastoral work involves Native Americans, African Americans, Hispanics, or other cultural groups residing in this country and abroad. At the root of these reflections lies the significance of symbolic communication, the essence of culture.

Father Zuern considers culture in a diagram of three concentric circles. A *center of intangibles*, the first circle, is at the heart of the diagram and represents the meaning level of that culture: its myths and symbols, its values and principles, its fundamental questions and the answers of that culture to those questions. Around the center of intangibles appears the *circle of structures*, which represents "the structures which underlie all the social institutions within a cultural society." These structures, simple or complex as they may be, provide the group with the means to confront and solve the most significant issues about living. Other circumstances that affect the group, such as, for example, the group's history and the environment that surrounds it, also influence these structures. The outer circle lies around this circle; it appears as the *circumference of tangibles*, namely, the visible, tangible elements of a culture, those signs and symbols through which the culture itself finds expression and by which other cultures merely begin to perceive it.

In this article Zuern proceeds to raise some questions about the way we all perceive cultures: Is it merely from the outward, outer level, that is, superficially? Or, rather, should we not attempt, at least, to penetrate all levels and come to know the culture from its "intangible," not evident, perspective? The answer to such a question is quite significant for all pastoral ministers committed to service in the Church today, particularly for liturgists and musicians, the poets of our postindustrial era who dare transform the intangible reality of the Risen Christ into tangible words, melodies, and songs through which the faithful can come to worship God in community.

I maintain that herein lies the difference between seeing ourselves and others as *tourists* (merely touching each other's outward layer) or as *pilgrims*, willing to learn more about one another's thoughts, feelings, and expressions and to respect the differences we discover precisely because a common vision and a common memory binds us together. I admit, nonetheless, that Zuern's simple yet provocative thoughts can raise other questions that may need answers. As we recall his three concentric circles, we can ask ourselves: Where in these circles do we place "language"? As we evaluate the language we utilize in our verbal communication with one another, we may uncover a few choices: the language of communication, which aims at orienting others to their whereabouts; the economic language of business or the manipulative language of politics, prevalent in so many societies; or the language of myths and symbols, which speak from and to the heart and becomes in all cultural groups the language of faith.

We would probably conclude that language must run through all three circles in each culture, although we may insist on preserving certain distinctions. Since the Second Vatican Council we have moved, for instance, from making our liturgical language one of rubrics and directives; but on the other hand, we can turn it into neither the language of business or politics, nor that of dogma or catechesis. The liturgical reform has challenged us to learn to speak the language of God and church and to express it in simple yet poetic ways for contemporary society. What have we actually done with language in the liturgy? What can we do in the future? Do we translate and express texts in the language of tourists, intellectuals, and strangers, or have we learned to promote in our celebrations the language of pilgrims, a language that leads its listeners to experience the salvific presence of God in history and to long for that presence in sacramental signs? What about music? Where does it belong? Where have we placed it? Where can we place it in the future? Perhaps if we learn to sing in one another's vernacular, so to speak, we may finally begin to know and love one another better.

Music in Catholic worship is an instrumental symbol, never intended for dominance but for support. Music, however, not only evokes in those who worship a deeper reality but also places them in touch with the same reality that has gathered them together. In liturgy, of course, this reality is none other than the Paschal Mystery, the process of dying and rising in Jesus, which we have all embraced from the moment of baptism and which we celebrate continually in our pilgrimage to the Father.

By the same token, in Catholic worship the reality of the Paschal Mystery assumes diverse features, languages, and styles. Through the liturgy of the Church in all parts of our world, the intangible reality of a God-made-unconditional-love in Jesus Christ becomes tangible in the lives and prayers of multiple communities who share the one Lord and the same faith because of a common baptism. This embrace between the Word and the cultures of our world defines the nature of our Catholic community, and simultaneously challenges us to preserve our unity in faith while celebrating the blessings of the Spirit in diverse forms.

We live in a "satellite age," when all world events seem to find a way to the minds and hearts of people through varied styles of communication. Despite this "satellite age," however, we gather to celebrate the presence of our Risen Lord in small communities filled with richness and variety. At communal prayer, when Christians lift up their hearts to the Lord, the symbol of music echoes the joys, sufferings, hopes, and dreams of the faithful who blend their voices with the voice of God the biblical texts reveal. At those moments God, as Good News, finds a way to the hearts of all people and, more powerful than a satellite human hands have made, never fails to call them to renewal and reconciliation, to compassion and forgiveness. God calls them to unveil in tangible ways the intangible power of God's presence.

Hispanic liturgy in the United States

The Catholic Church in the United States enjoys a privileged gift of the presence of a multiplicity of Catholic communities, which bring to the "whole" of North American Catholicism the uniqueness of their cultural and religious expressions. However, I must primarily focus on Hispanic worship expressions, specifically music, though I feel that we cannot ignore how much interaction among all cultural groups takes place in this complex society each day.

Hispanic Catholics in the United States constitute a composite of cultural traditions that, though rooted historically in Spain's evangelization of the Americas, has developed over the centuries unique characteristics. The Catholic Church in this country has witnessed a display of these characteristics particularly, though not exclusively, in large urban centers where representative families from Mexico, Central and South America, the Caribbean islands, and even from Brazil, Portugal, and Spain itself have settled to become part of the larger, complex, North American society without losing their unique cultural identity.

Integrated, though not assimilated, these families, which worship in spirit and truth, experience a twofold dynamic. On one side they fear the disintegration of family values as a result of social strains that lead their youth away from God and church toward a depressing secularism that markets primarily a spirit of consumerism and relativism. On the other hand, they wish to express their faith in Jesus, the Church, Mary, and the saints in ways that can help them liberate themselves and their children from those strains and journey to happiness and peace. They live in this country not as tourists but as pilgrims, whose journey of faith and love is positively contagious to other cultural groups and unreservedly "catholic" in the best possible description of this term. At times, however, and under specific circumstances, they have suffered the misunderstanding and the oppression of specific local groups, even Church leaders, that have led them away from the church of their initiation into other ecclesial congregations, syncretisms, or sects foreign to their heritage but rich in hospitality and understanding.

The cultural pluralism the Second Vatican Council provided in its theological renewal and liturgical reforms, and the spirit in which the reforms have evolved over the last thirty years, facilitate for Hispanic Catholics a medium in which they can contribute with their gifts and talents to the spiritual growth of all Catholics. It also provides an opportunity to ensure Hispanics' own Catholic and cultural identity in the midst of rapid and complex social changes.

From the many elements that comprise the reformed vision of Vatican II and subsequent synods, liturgy and spirituality need to become for all Catholics, in this case Hispanic Catholics living in the United States, the backbone, the fountain from which their lives find meaning and the summit toward which their hearts must journey. Music, and specifically liturgical and religious music, has indeed become an integral component of this process.

In 1982, the Instituto Nacional Hispano de Liturgia, Inc. undertook to study the structure of the Mass among representative Hispanic communities in the United States. The U.S. Bishops' Committee on the Liturgy had commissioned this study and challenged the Instituto, in collaboration with the Federation of Diocesan Liturgical Commissions, to assess the range of Hispanic responses to current liturgical reforms. The project began on the eve of the twentieth anniversary of Vatican II's promulgation of the *Constitution on the Sacred Liturgy*.

While the process used for the study, which involved a random sample of over six hundred Hispanics of Mexican American, Puerto Rican, Cuban, and other ethnic backgrounds, has been published in various periodicals, the results that emerged out of the study continue to shape the agenda of Instituto board meetings and that of other pastoral organizations committed to Hispanic ministry in the country.

Almost unanimously, the participants made liturgical music their first priority. Hispanic assemblies continue to make music their most important avenue of expression in worship today. Melody, rhythm, and lyrics blend to provide communitarian expression to a people whose religious roots are universal and, at the same time, imbued with specific life experiences. In and through the musical expression of Hispanic Catholics, the hopeful features of a pilgrim people display both the suffering and the joy of Jesus and his church.

Spanish liturgical music in Hispanic worship

In the context of our current reflection, then, we must place the variety of Hispanic assemblies of the country and display, through their repertoire, both the aesthetic and textual strengths of their compositions, as well as the differences in rhythms and styles that characterize them.

Preliminary to the presentation of this repertoire, one needs to make the following observations.

1. There is a markedly different style of church experience, and thus church music, between the Eastern Seaboard of the United States and the West. The original division provided by the Office of Hispanic Affairs of the bishops' conference established eight different regions. Members of each region compose the Instituto's board and have served the bishops of those regions in implementing liturgical reform among Hispanic Catholics and in promoting avenues of inculturation with Hispanic assemblies.

2. The liturgical music of each region has been used at national conventions the Instituto sponsored, as well as at the Spanish tracks the National Pastoral Musicians' conventions sponsored regionally or nationally. Hispanic Catholics from all regions have learned to sing with one another and pray with one another.

3. Musically, the western section of the United States seems to display a definite Mexican rhythm, which extends from California through Texas and into the Midwestern region of the country. Exception must be made for a New Mexican or Southwestern style of music, which points to Spain and its missionaries there as the root of their musical expression.

4. The eastern section of the United States seems to experience a strong Caribbean emphasis in musical styles of worship, due primarily to the cultural and religious experience of Catholics from Puerto Rico and the Dominican Republic in the Northeast and from Cuba in the Southeast. In the future, this difference between East and West may not be so marked due to the influx of Mexican and Central

American migratory groups in areas of the Northeast (New York) and the Southeast (the Carolinas and Georgia).

5. While the music of Spain seemed to have influenced the worship experience of all of these communities during the first decades of the liturgical reform, original music local musicians composed seems to surface more frequently today as the reform has begun to affect Hispanic Catholic assemblies at prayer. This evolutionary process, nonetheless, does not mean to exclude all liturgical music from Spain, but rather motivates Hispanic Catholics in the United States to see in music the symbol that speaks to and from their hearts and their integrated cultural experience at the "center of their intangibles."

6. Despite what some non-Hispanic individuals may think or feel as they observe the cultural experience of Hispanics from the "outward circumference of tangibles," neither Spanish language nor worshiping in Spanish is a problem for Hispanic Catholics in this country, though we all must admit that there exists among the Hispanic regions a variety of language nuances in the use of Spanish and definite preferences of musical styles. We discover this same variety and these preferences, of course, in the regionalism of most of the countries of the world.

7. In summary, then, for anyone to address this topic to such a universal audience, a diverse repertoire must always be present to include selections from the following areas that represent diverse assemblies: New Mexico, Texas, California, the Northwest, the Northeast, and the Southeast of the United States; subculturally speaking, from Spanish-Mexico, Tex-Mex (Texas-Mexican), the Californian sound, the Northwestern sound, Puerto Rico, the Dominican Republic, and Cuba. Our contention is always the same in each case: The liturgical music of these assemblies reflects not only the unique church experience of those who worship in that area, but also a longing to sing with one another as one pilgrim community bound by a common origin and a common purpose in Christ.

Concluding remarks

I venture to offer these conclusions, which aim to become only my personal perception of the state of Hispanic liturgical music in the United States:

1. We have finally moved from the exclusive use of liturgical music from Spain to the composition, publication, and interpretation of

music composed in Spanish-speaking countries outside of the United States and by Hispanics in the United States. Several reasons may be attributed to this change:

a) The increased awareness of Hispanic heritage as a gift and not as a threat to North American society (as the pastoral letter of our bishops described several years ago and to which the various *Encuentros Nacionales* of the last two decades witnessed).

b) The increased participation of Hispanic communities as Hispanic assemblies in parishes and dioceses throughout the country and the revolutionary impact that the discovery of scripture has brought about in individual Catholics after the Second Vatican Council.

c) The efforts of national organizations and regional corporations that have become committed to the publication of Hispanic liturgical materials and have taken financial risks to serve our Hispanic assemblies. Besides the Instituto Nacional Hispano de Liturgia, a few others need to be mentioned: historically, the Benzinger publishing house, no longer in existence, and, currently, Oregon Catholic Press, Liturgy Training Publications, and World Library Publications.

2. These local compositions reflect the different ecclesial realities that constitute the assemblies that sing them:

a) Many Hispanic Catholics, with the new wave of immigration of the last thirty years, find in the rhythms of their country of origin (as well as in the religious festivals that provide the framework for this music) an avenue of social adaptation in a new setting that, different from their own, causes multiple strains on their religious experience. Music, as a symbol, assists them to experience the healing touch of their heritage and allows them to move forward in their process of integration into North America society.

b) Most Hispanic Catholics, however, who have already dwelled in North American territory for centuries, mostly in the Western and Southwestern regions, enjoy the music of their country of origin, namely Mexico, or, in some cases, Central America, perhaps because it echoes for them the joyful heritage from which they come more than the need for social adaptation in the present. While this assertion appears to be true, many families strongly fear that most of their youngsters tend to reject their Hispanic heritage and feel disoriented and confused. Yet, Hispanic traditions seem to remain through music (e.g., young mariachi groups surface everywhere).

c) Even so, one cannot speak of Hispanic Catholic liturgical or musical experience in the United States in a uniform manner. Though of one people, united by a common language and tradition, these assemblies express their faith in slightly different ways as they bring to the liturgy of the Church a variety of ecclesial realities. One of these realities, ever-present in the Southwest, is that of bilingual celebrations.

3. A word about so-called bilingual music. Some claim that bilingual music provides the answer for Hispanic Catholics in the United States. Although the concept is not unique to this country and even to the Church, current efforts fail to grasp the uniqueness of the concept. One may describe what we hear now—and unfortunately what some assemblies have embraced without any constructive critique—as Spanish texts fitted into North American musical modes or styles, which speak to the heart of North Americans sensitive to Hispanic ministry, and to some bilingual communities, but not to all.

a) Composers must grow careful of the use of the Spanish language in music, particularly the consistency and balance of the Spanish accent with the musical accents of the melodies they compose.

b) I believe that to become an authentic expression of the assembly, bilingual music must first emerge out of the theological, social, and liturgical reflection of bilingual or multicultural communities. At that level a choice must be made whether community members will make an effort to sing in one another's language and musical styles, or combine them in a creative manner.

c) At the present time, bilingual or multilingual texts function better as verses of an antiphonal composition that maintains a dominant language in its antiphons, much like the style Taizé provides.

4. Lastly, Hispanic Catholics enjoy praying with and singing in the musical styles of other cultural groups that constitute the Church in the United States. They find no difficulty in forming part of a mosaic of cultures and joining in the rich tradition of hymnody prevalent in many Anglo assemblies or the moving rhythmical spirituals of African American communities. I feel they are even open to learn more about the Asian experience, which seems to grow considerably in California, Houston, New Orleans, Brooklyn, and other parts of the country.

Their only hope is this: Can others come to know them as well through the vehicle of liturgical music and sing with them the hope of a new life without oppression, prejudice, or resentment? The Church and our faith provide the framework for such hope. And as this hope materializes in all of our Catholic assemblies of the United States, the kingdom of Jesus Christ will become more evident to all.

Father Sosa gave this address to the members of Universa Laus *who gathered in Connecticut in August of 1999 at its annual meeting.* Universa Laus *is an international organization of liturgical musicians.*

PART V

Preaching

PREACHING IN SPANISH:
SYMBOLS AND *SATOS*
Kenneth G. Davis, OFM Conv. and Rev. David G. Sánchez

The Catholic Church in the United States is experiencing a new era in crosscultural worship. Increasingly, priests preach crossculturally, especially in Spanish. Their homiletic training, however, typically has been in English and generally has used only white, male methodologies. Different assemblies require that preachers use different approaches for their homilies.

We find the following method useful in preaching with Hispanic communities. It both appropriates certain elements of current homiletic methods and also critiques them based on crosscultural experience.

The assembly

Hispanic is actually an inadequate term for assemblies that speak Spanish, because the word refers to a population from twenty-one different countries—each with a distinct history and culture. One adjective for this diverse group of people is the Puerto Rican expression *sato*. Dr. Loida I. Martell-Otero says:

> A sata/o is one who is not pure. . . . They are unwanted . . . This term . . . represents well the experience of many U.S. Hispanics/Latinos who live in the United States. They are stereotyped, rejected, insulted. They are relegated to the periphery of society, to the bottom rung of society (Martell-Otero, 8–9).

The assembly in the Spanish-speaking Church is a congregation of *Satos*, and although diverse, they share one common experience: social dislocation. Cubans are exiles, Chicanos were conquered, Central and South Americans flee economic collapse or political turmoil. Like an injured joint, each member of this body of Christ shares the common experience of feeling out of place.

Among Puerto Ricans, however, the word *sato* also has positive connotations. *Satos* are not just victims, but survivors. *Satos* can survive through faith and thrive through holiness. This is the good news this community needs to hear. Proclaiming the Good News within that reality requires a new homiletic mentality.

Typical homiletic methods

Culture as well as faith shapes preaching. Preaching in a new social or cultural location requires experimentation with new styles. For Catholics before the Second Vatican Council, deductive and didactic sermons prevailed. Preachers proposed a theme and then analyzed it. Listeners never speculated about the conclusion because the preacher had affirmed it at the beginning.

After Vatican II, inductive preaching became more accepted, and after the publication of *Fulfilled in Your Hearing*, the U.S. Catholic bishops' 1983 document on preaching, narrative methods became popular. Although this approach often includes stories, narrative methods use plot as the actual vehicle for the message. Narrative homilies, however, are still rather literal and episodic (i.e., they have a determined climax and conclusion) because the dynamics of discourse drive them. Homilists underutilize graphics (even contemporary media). In the narrative method, they may creatively construct, shape, and discipline metaphors, but too often they ignore sensory images.

Symbolic communication

In a community of *Satos*, however, elaborate and somatic images are traditional vehicles for proclaiming the faith. Because these symbols are physical, they are open to both children and adults, the educated as well as the unlettered. And because they are dynamic and communal, they express traditions in ways that both respect *Sato* differences and also unite them in a common faith.

Symbols are fundamental to preaching with *Satos* because these same symbols are elemental to their particular spirituality. Precisely because they have often been abandoned at the margins of Church and society, *Satos* have not always had a sufficient number of ordained preachers or equal access to the sacraments. Their spirituality, therefore, grew less from the Mass and more from the masses; leadership was lay and often female. Instead of sermons and sacraments, images of saints and Marian processions marked the tempo of life and defined their worldview. Even today people respond most to those liturgies that include material symbols such as the cool touch of water, the gritty feel of ashes, and the warm presence of candles.

The context of our preaching (liturgy) already includes such symbols. Why not integrate those sensory images into that preaching? Mary Birmingham's *Word and Worship Workbook* series suggests this very integration. She rightly claims that symbols give identity. Orlando Espín and others assert exactly this insight when they speak of the importance of Hispanic popular religion. By *popular* they do not mean "faddish" but rather "constitutive of a people." Religion literally means to "tie together"; popular religion is the spiritual symbol system that unites and celebrates a particular cultural community and gives it an identity. Preaching to such a community must therefore convoke those symbols that evoke their God.

Both a story *and* a symbol might elicit the good news of God's presence in a *Sato* community. Symbols communicate the tradition from which they come and also connect to a temporal and spatial reality where the preaching event is actually experienced. The challenge for the preacher is both to stir the daily reality of the *Sato* and also arouse the power of symbol so that the two jointly enlighten each other. In this way, the life of the assembly becomes a reference for reverence.

A method for preaching

What would happen if during Advent a preacher juxtaposed an image of the Holy Family and their flight to Egypt with a story about an undocumented family crossing the desert? Would a *Sato* assembly reminisce about the solidarity of God while they recall their identification with the Holy Family? Would such a graphic recollection motivate them to see how they are part of the story of salvation? While never ignoring the Lectionary readings, the goal of the preacher is not so much to demonstrate a connection among the readings as to quicken an experiential connection between the proclamation and the people. Symbols can induce such liturgical labor.

Instead of relating *Chicken Soup for the Soul*-type stories to scripture, could not a contextual symbol animate the relationship that is always extant between *Satos* and scripture? Why use fiction when the factual drama of an assembly's experience is already expectant with the passion, death, and resurrection that groans to be midwifed through their liturgical symbols?

Nonverbal silences, pauses, facial expressions, and body language enliven narrative preaching. Could not the liturgical symbols that surround our preaching become central rather than peripheral, so that possibilities and choices that may not even occur to the preacher could birth God in surprising, empowering, and liberating ways through the complex and intuitive experience of *Sato* symbols? Such twinning of word discourse and non-discursive symbol would thus open the preaching experience itself to greater participation by the assembly.

One easy example of the use of *Sato* symbols is the *Posadas* (literally "lodging"), the Advent celebration of the Holy Family's search for shelter in Bethlehem. Traditionally, one group outside the dark church with the Holy Family knocks and pleads to enter. Those inside refuse. Eventually, amid chants of "Welcome, pilgrims," the doors are opened, the church is lighted, and those outside enter.

This traditional and dramatic symbol experience wedded to a homily could include verses of the song used as a commentary on the day's scripture. The preacher could interview the Holy Family or question participants about boundaries and thresholds, darkness and light, hospitality and hostility. Like other catalysts, this suggested homiletic mode may explode, but a controlled although sometimes surprising explosion through the careful ordering of symbol and word is what preserves this homiletic formula from becoming formulaic.

Revelatory symbols

Preaching to *Satos* is not to be a chaotic combination of symbols left to individual interpretations. While robust symbols speak for themselves, proper appropriation provokes a Christian appreciation of mediation rather than the magic of symbiotic association. Mary Birmingham discusses different kinds of symbols, but enumerates nine liturgical ones: water, light/fire, word, garments, oil/spirit, hands, bread/wine, community, and cross. Each is a liturgical expectation preachers too often ignore.

Symbolic imagery abounds in *Sato* spirituality as well. Because most communication is nonverbal, perhaps *Satos* can teach homilists how to expand the concept of preaching to include forms of communication beyond words alone. Although scripture uniquely reveals God, preaching could be a more sacramental encounter with God if it incorporated appropriate sense-symbols.

The homiletic challenge is to render familiar symbols so that they tender not only a discreet, distant past but also the assembly's unique present. The book *Preaching and Culture in Latino Congregations* posits the idea of preparation between preacher and the base community. Mary Birmingham gives a format that provides details for such cooperation. With such preparation, a homilist can coordinate a liturgy with ministers of music and environment that delights the eye while instructing the ear, breathes divinity while touching humanity, and motivates unity while tasting diversity.

Sato preachers may need to adapt some of the symbols Birmingham identified. A bare cross may be too sanitary a symbol for a community writhing on the crucifix of prejudice. Divine floods cleansing evil may be the water symbol needed by survivors of institutionalized violence that human justice never redressed. Certainly the Mother of God is a fixed liturgical symbol of Satos. Moreover, each Hispanic community has its own peculiar liturgical symbols. A godparent tosses coins after an infant baptism; a fifteen-year-old dons the garments of a princess; a groom spills arras (thirteen wedding coins) into his bride's hands; and a roadside cross marks violent death. When preaching with Satos, all the symbols of la religiosidad popular ("popular religion") are sacred texts that preachers must consult as necessary commentaries on sacred scripture.

Proper use of symbol can mold and model the sermon. Pablo Jiménez suggests proclaiming parallels between the experience of the people of God in the Bible and the experience of the people of God in the barrio. And Justo González insists that such proclamation in Spanish must necessarily include experiences of survivors. Alone such words instruct, but, collaborating with Sato symbols, they conspire to inspire.

Conclusion

Preaching with Satos requires the attention of contemporary homiletics. To learn Spanish is not the only challenge; another is to appreciate the cultural idioms expressed in symbols as well as language. A method of exploring, elaborating, even embroidering the homily through nondiscursive symbol may be as important to preaching in Spanish as nonverbal communication is to the narrative method English so often employs. This perspective presents a new challenge for homiletics. But for the Sato community, sensory symbols may be the best way to give tongue to their God who, like symbols themselves, is always ultimately unknowable yet by no means unknown, always mysterious yet in no way nameless, forever transcendent although never anonymous.

The authors thank Allan Figueroa Deck, SJ, Guerric DeBona, OSB, and Richard Stern, EdD for their help with this article.

References

Birmingham, Mary. *Word and Worship Workbook: For Ministry in Initiation, Preaching, Religious Education, and Formation.* New York: Paulist Press, 1998, 2000.

Bishops' Committee on Priestly Life and Ministry. *Fulfilled in Your Hearing: The Homily and the Sunday Assembly.* Washington, DC: United States Catholic Conference, 1983.

Bonnot, Bernard R., Thomas Boomershine, and Brian Sweeney. "A Liturgical Via Media." *America* 185, November 5, 2001.

Costas, Orlando. *Comunicación por Medio de la Predicación.* Miami: Editorial Caribe, 1989.

Davis, Kenneth G. "Cross-Cultural Preaching." *Chicago Studies* 39, no. 3 (Winter 2000): 233–253.

———. "Preaching in Spanish as a Second Language." *Homiletic* XVII (Summer 1992): 7–10.

Davis, Kenneth G., ed. *Misa, Mesa, y Musa: Liturgy in the U.S. Hispanic Church.* Schiller Park, Illinois: World Library Publications, 1997.

Davis, Kenneth G. and Jorge Presmanes, eds. *Preaching and Culture in Latino Congregations.* Chicago: Liturgy Training Publications, 2000.

Espín, Orlando O. *The Faith of the People: Theological Reflections on Popular Catholicism.* Maryknoll, New York: Orbis Books, 1997.

Francis, Mark R. and Arturo Pérez Rodríguez. *Primero Dios: Hispanic Liturgical Resources.* Chicago: Liturgy Training Publications, 1997.

González, Justo L. "Reading Ourselves in Spanish." *Apuntes* 17, no. 1 (Spring 1997): 12–17.

Jiménez, Pablo. "From Text to Sermon." *Apuntes* 17, no. 2 (Summer 1997): 35–40.

Martell-Otero, Loida I. "Of *Satos* and Saints: Salvation from the Periphery." *Perspectivas: Occasional Papers.* Princeton, NJ: Hispanic Theological Initiative, 4, Summer 2001.

Pagan, Samuel. *Púlpito, Teología y Esperanza.* Miami: Editorial Caribe, 1988.

Pérez-Rodríguez, Arturo and Mark R. Francis, eds. *Los Documentos Litúrgicos.* Chicago: Liturgy Training Publications, 1997.

Romero, C. Gilbert. *Hispanic Devotional Piety: Tracing the Biblical Roots.* Maryknoll, New York: Orbis Books, 1991.

THE THEOLOGY OF GUADALUPE:
AN INTRODUCTION FOR PREACHERS
AND PASTORAL MINISTERS
Timothy Matovina

"I welcome with joy the proposal of the synod fathers that the feast of Our Lady of Guadalupe, mother and evangelizer of America, be celebrated throughout the continent on December 12."
—Pope John Paul II, *Ecclesia in America* (no. 11)

Years ago I attended the seventieth wedding anniversary of Doña Manuela and Don José, who had been married during the Mexican Revolution. The church was packed with their friends, relatives, children, grandchildren, great-grandchildren, and even two great-great-grandchildren. After Communion Doña Manuela rolled her husband in his wheelchair to a side altar of Our Lady of Guadalupe. Holding his hand and gazing into Guadalupe's eyes, she uttered a prayer in Spanish that she probably intended to be private but was audible throughout the hushed congregation. "*Virgencita linda,*" she began as she poured out her soul to her celestial mother and thanked Guadalupe for her family and the joys, blessings, and help during hardships over many years. Her lengthy prayer was punctuated with a self-made litany to Guadalupe which included invocations such as "*Tú, quien eres la madre de todos* [you, who are the mother of all] . . . *que nunca nos abandonas* [who never abandons us] . . . *quien nos acompaña en nuestros dolores* [who accompanies us in our sorrows] . . . ."

But what I remember most was the touching way Doña Manuela finished her prayer. She told Guadalupe that she had tried to be the best mother she could, but that soon she and her husband would not be in this world. Then she passed the mantle of her own motherhood back to Guadalupe: "*Yo he sido la madre de esta familia para unos pocos años, pero tú eres la madre de todos para siempre. Cuídales a éstos, tus hijos, cuando Dios ya me llame de este mundo* [I have been the mother of this family for but a few years, but you are the mother of all forever. Care for these your children when God calls me from this world]."

Countless devotees like Doña Manuela have long revered Our Lady of Guadalupe as their cherished *madre querida*. Homilists, theologians, pastoral leaders, and devotees themselves have also contended for centuries that Guadalupe's meaning begins with her maternal love, but by no means ends there. Collectively, these commentators have drawn on three primary sources for their analyses: the Guadalupe apparitions narrative, the image itself, and the expressions of devotion offered to her. Theological reflections on these sources provide helpful insights for those charged with preaching or preparing liturgies for the Guadalupe feast, as well as others who engage Guadalupe in their respective ministries.

The apparitions narrative

The Náhuatl Guadalupe apparitions narrative, the *Nican Mopohua* (a title derived from the document's first words, "Here we recount"), is a source of enduring fascination and theological reflection. For Guadalupan devotees, the *Nican Mopohua* is the foundational text that recounts the 1531 Guadalupe apparitions to the Indigenous neophyte Juan Diego (whom Pope John Paul II canonized in July, 2002). As every Guadalupano knows, the *Nican Mopohua* narrates how Guadalupe sent Juan Diego to request that Juan de Zumárraga, the first bishop of Mexico, build a temple on the hill of Tepeyac in her honor. At first the bishop doubted, but came to believe when Juan Diego presented him exquisite flowers that were out of season, and the image of Guadalupe miraculously appeared on the humble *indio*'s *tilma* (cloak). In various ways Guadalupe provided Juan Diego with hope and consolation, including the healing of his uncle, Juan Bernardino. Numerous commentators have reflected profoundly on the *Nican Mopohua*'s significance for understanding, living, and announcing the Christian message in the Americas. Their meditations frequently take into account the historical context of sixteenth-century Mesoamerica, especially the tumultuous effects of European conquest on the Indigenous peoples.

The theme contemporary theologians have articulated most frequently concerning the Guadalupe narrative is that of justice or liberation, the breaking in of God's reign that upends the status quo: in the words of Mary's Magnificat, the way God "has deposed the mighty from their thrones and raised the lowly to high places" (Luke 1:52). In this interpretation the larger context of Spanish conquest is particularly important. Hernán Cortés led the forces that conquered the Aztec capital Tenochtitlan (now Mexico City) in 1521. The attempt to destroy or alter all things Indigenous followed military victory: the Aztec's political and economic systems, dress, customs, habits, language, religion, and, intentionally or not, their sense of worth and purpose in life.

In this context, the Guadalupe event is a counter-narrative to the complete defeat of the native peoples. Guadalupe's first words to Juan Diego are "Dignified Juan, dignified Juan Diego." She then goes on to give him the mission of communicating to Bishop Zumárraga her desire that a temple be built on the hill of Tepeyac where she "will show and give to all people all my love, my compassion, my help, and my protection." Juan Diego's joyful confidence is soon crushed, however, as he waits an extended time before being allowed to see the clearly incredulous bishop. After a series of further encounters with Guadalupe and interviews with the bishop, the story reaches its climax: The doubting bishop believes when Juan Diego drops flowers that grew out of season from his *tilma* and presents the image of Guadalupe miraculously appearing on the rough cloth of his cloak.

Guadalupe's words of comfort and calling effect the narrative's dramatic reversals. At the beginning only Guadalupe trusts Juan Diego; by the end the bishop and his assistants believe he is truly her messenger. At the outset Juan Diego stands meekly before the bishop; in the end the stooped *indio* stands erect while the bishop and his household kneel before him and venerate the image on his *tilma*. Throughout the account Juan Diego must journey to the center of the city from Tepeyac some three miles to the north; at the end of the narration the bishop and his entourage accompany Juan Diego to Tepeyac, where they will build the temple Guadalupe requested.

Symbolically, the presence of ecclesial leadership and the church they are constructing thus move from the center of their capital city out to the margins among the Indigenous people. Thus the narrative encompasses the powerful message that discipleship requires listening to the voices of the forgotten and the marginalized, defending and helping them to sense their dignity as God's sons and daughters, and preferentially choosing them as the recipients of the Church's proclamation of the gospel, service, and struggle for a more just social order. The ongoing meaning of these dramatic reversals for Christian believers was eloquently expressed in a Guadalupan homily I heard that challenged congregants: "We cannot love Our Lady of Guadalupe unless we love *el pobre* [the poor one] Juan Diego with the commitment of our lives."

The Theology of Guadalupe ————————————————— **103**

A complementary theme in the Guadalupe story is the theology of conversion it narrates. Bishop Zumárraga is called beyond the blindness of ethnocentrism and pride so embedded in the mentality of the Spanish conquerors. To his credit, he comes to recognize the truth of the message Juan Diego announces and the *indio*'s dignity as a child of God Guadalupe called. This recognition required a radical conversion on his part to overcome the biases and limitations of his Spanish culture and hear the voice of God's mother speaking to him through a most unexpected messenger.

Juan Diego, on the other hand, did not need to be converted from excessive pride. On the contrary, in the *Nican Mopohua* his greatest sin is a lack of self-worth, an internalization of the effects of the conquest, particularly the conquerors' presumption that the natives were inferior or even subhuman. Ultimately Juan Diego's internalization of the conquerors' judgments and stereotypes led him to fail to accept fully that he, too, was made in God's image and likeness. In one of the narrative's most moving passages, he returns to Guadalupe after his first interview with the bishop and asks her to send another messenger "who is respected and esteemed," because he is too lowly and unimportant; she has sent him "to a place where I do not belong." Her response is tender but firm:

> Listen, my most abandoned son, know well in your heart that there are not a few of my servants and messengers to whom I could give the mandate of taking my thought and my word so that my will may be accomplished. But it is absolutely necessary that you personally go and speak about this, and that precisely through your mediation and help, my wish and my desire be realized (*Nican Mopohua*).

The conversion of Juan Diego—and by extension the call to conversion of all the conquered native peoples and anyone else who doubts their own fundamental goodness as a creation of God—is not a call from sinful pride to humble acceptance of God's will. It is a call from debilitating self-abasement to a healthy embrace of God's love and the mission of living for God and others to which that love beckons us. Thus the pathway of conversion is not the same for all, though the call to conversion and transformation extends to each. We are all called to see ourselves and others as God and blessed Mary of

Guadalupe see us: precious, dignified, and made in God's own image and likeness. But we are also called to confront our sinful pride and spiritual blindness, the Juan de Zumárraga tendencies that lurk inside each of us. Christian conversion demands that we follow the pathways of both Juan Diego and of Juan de Zumárraga.

The profound conversions the *Nican Mopohua* recounted lead to another major theological theme, that of reconciliation. One of the most striking elements of this story is that, as Juan Diego is lifted up and Bishop Zumárraga humbles himself, the two meet in the middle as brothers. This reversal is even more striking when one thinks of the strong language of the Magnificat: "The hungry he has given every good thing, while the rich he has sent empty away" (Luke 1:53). In the theological vision of the Guadalupe narrative, the seemingly complete reversal of the Magnificat is tempered: Guadalupe does not give all to Juan Diego and leave Juan de Zumárraga as one who is "sent empty away," but gives each according to his need. Her promise to care for "all people" is meant for the conquerors, the conquered, those brought over as slaves, immigrants, and all children born of unions in this "new" land.

The process of reconciliation is never easy, as the ongoing chasms and hostilities between different races, social classes, genders, and other human groupings clearly reveal. It requires honest admissions of sins and failures, true contrition, the willingness to forgive on the part of the offended party, acts of reparation that make amends for wrongdoing and demonstrate sorrow for offenses, and the concerted effort to sin no more. But the Guadalupe narrative inspires us to see the difficult pathway of conversion and reconciliation as a road we can walk together in grace and joy.

Another theme, evangelization, is doubly present in the *Nican Mopohua*. First Our Lady of Guadalupe evangelized Juan Diego, and then she empowered him to evangelize others. Guadalupe is not an evangelizer who scares or coerces, but one who wins Juan Diego's heart with the love and compassion of God, calls him to a mission, and then supports him and assures him that he can do great things for her and for God. Because of the testimony of Juan Diego, not only was the bishop convinced, but "the entire city was deeply moved; they came to see and admire her precious image." Juan Diego is transformed from one who hears the word to one who announces it, from one who feels unworthy to one who boldly proclaims Guadalupe's message, from a neophyte to an empowered evangelizer. The Guadalupe narrative emphatically reminds pastoral leaders that it is not enough that the Juan Diegos of this world hear the gospel. Rather, the narrative teaches us that when the poor and marginalized evangelize one another, as well as pastoral leaders, evangelization has begun to flourish.

As the Guadalupe feast has gained greater prominence, yet another theme has grown in importance: the connection between the apparitions narrative, the feast day readings, and the Advent season in which the Guadalupe feast falls. In 1754, Pope Benedict XIV established December 12 as the date for her feast; at the request of the Special Assembly for America of the Synod of Bishops, Pope John Paul II declared it an official liturgical feast for all the Americas in 1999. Along with the general option of choosing readings for the Guadalupe feast from the Common of the Blessed Virgin Mary, the Lectionary used in the United States has specific options for the Gospel and the first reading that are clearly consistent with the Advent theme of joyfully awaiting the Lord's coming: the Annunciation (Luke 1:26–38), the Visitation, with the first line of the Magnificat (Luke 1:39–47); and Zechariah 2:14–17, which begins, "Sing and rejoice, O daughter Zion! See, I am coming to dwell among you, says the Lord." Many parishes dramatically reenact the Guadalupe apparitions, sometimes after Mass but often after the Gospel, allowing for the incorporation of the story of the apparitions into the homily. For example, one homilist I heard declared that, just as Mary visited Elizabeth and shared the good news of Christ, so Guadalupe visited Juan Diego—and through him the peoples of America—to bring her maternal love and the good news of her son. The homilist then called us to live the spirituality of Advent: awaiting the coming of Christ in joy as Mary and her kinswoman Elizabeth did, and announcing the good news of his coming as Our Lady of Guadalupe did to Juan Diego and he in turn did to others.

Image and devotion

Theologians have shown that the image of Guadalupe combines elements from both the Iberian Catholic and Aztec cultures, forming what pastor and theologian Virgilio Elizondo deems "the gospel on native cloth." The symbolic meaning of the Guadalupe image itself has also long been a source of fascination and reflection. For example, the moon under her feet and the rays of the sun that emanate from behind her recall the Aztec gods of the sun and moon (to this day one can still see the great pyramids of the sun and moon gods at Teotihuacán near Mexico City). Unlike the Spanish conquerors, Guadalupe does not destroy these reminders of Aztec belief but stands on the moon and blocks out the sun as a sign that she brings something newer and greater to fulfill the native peoples' spiritual longings. One can interpret the stars on her mantle as a new age dawning through her love and evangelizing message. Her eyes are looking down, showing that she is not a god, while her hands are folded in a native gesture of offering. The black band under her hands is said to be a maternity band, signifying that she bears a child who is to be born through her in the Americas. Yet the image as a whole also resembles European images of the Madonna, especially depictions of the Immaculate Conception common during the time of the Spanish colonization.

Together these and other elements of the Guadalupe image support an interpretation of Guadalupe as the Mother of God who proclaims Christ to the Americas, an announcement of the Christian gospel in a manner that respected native symbols and cultures even as it offered something new. Noting that Guadalupe is a mestiza—a person of mixed race who synthesizes the Aztec and Iberian worlds—Pope John Paul II stated that Guadalupe's image and message present "an impressive example of a perfectly inculturated evangelization." She is a model not only in the historical sense that "the appearance of Mary to the native Juan Diego on the hill of Tepeyac in 1531 had a decisive effect on evangelization," but continues as her "influence greatly overflows the boundaries of Mexico, spreading to the whole continent" (*Ecclesia in America*, no. 11).

Thus the image of Guadalupe teaches that evangelization—the mission of proclaiming Christ in word and deed to which all the baptized are called—is not effectively served when we impose our cultural ways as if they were intrinsic to the gospel, but when we creatively announce the gospel within the cultural context of the faith community we are accompanying. This task is never easy and always requires patience and discernment; Guadalupe exemplifies the ideal of respect for local cultures and faithfulness to the gospel for which we all strive.

Guadalupe's countenance has led to her association with the painful process of *mestizaje*, the dynamic and often violent mixing of cultures, religious systems, races, and peoples. Virgilio Elizondo asserts that Mexican Americans are mixed-race mestizos born from two dramatic clashes of peoples: first the Mesoamericans with the conquistadores of sixteenth-century Catholic Spain and then, in the century and a half following the U.S. takeover of northern Mexico, Mexican-descent residents with U.S. citizens and Catholics steeped in European roots. In his preaching and theological writings, Elizondo proclaims that Mexican Americans are thus the dignified bearers of a rich mestizo heritage—neither Spanish nor Indigenous, neither Mexican nor North American, but a dynamic mixture of all these root cultures.

Our Lady of Guadalupe, whom Elizondo describes as a "mestiza" and "the first truly American person and as such the mother of the new generations," provides hope and inspiration for Mexican Americans struggling to embrace their identity as mestizos, synthesize the richness from their parent cultures, and be transformative agents of Guadalupe's power to harmonize diverse peoples. Observing the multitudes who have found faith and compassion in "the mestiza face of the Virgin of Tepeyac," Pope John Paul II articulated similar insights. A seemingly minor but highly significant element of his teaching on Guadalupe was that she is a mother, queen, evangelizer, and patroness who calls all peoples of the hemisphere to form a united American continent. Note he did not speak of "America" in the plural, but in the singular.

This point accentuates a claim the pope first made in the hemisphere on his initial visit to the United States, when he boldly likened the split between the richer and more powerful nations and the more economically impoverished nations to the rich man and Lazarus of Luke 16. John Paul avowed that one of the great challenges today is to see the intrinsic link between the rich northern and poorer southern halves of the planet. Acclaiming Guadalupe as the mother and evangelizer of all America reminds us that all the peoples of America—North, South, Central, and the Caribbean—are daughters and sons of the same mother. Our destinies are intimately conjoined, and the mestiza face of Guadalupe both reminds us of the ties that bind us and challenges us to transcend narrow parochialism and nationalism to adopt a wider vision of our faith, our Church, and our calling as disciples.

Another important aspect of the Guadalupe image is that Guadalupe's daughters and sons constantly revel in her beauty. For numerous devotees the core experience of Guadalupe is the replication of Juan Diego's encounter with their celestial mother. As he did on the hill of Tepeyac, they stand before her. In innumerable conversations, prayers, and sustained gazes at her image, they relive Juan Diego's mystical encounter. What do they see in her face? According to many devotees, they see compassion, care, love, and a beauty that beckons her children to a greater sense of awe, wonder, gratitude, and faith. Here is a theology of beauty: the feeling of unmerited, gratuitous love that numerous devotees have experienced in their mother Guadalupe's eyes. This experience is not a call to conversion or discipleship based on fear or demands. It is an invitation to fuller life with God through the contemplation of beauty and a profound sense of gratitude, because I am loved for no other reason than that God is love and desires that all created beings reflect the immensity of divine goodness.

Both male and female devotees frequently acclaim Guadalupe as their mother. But, as one male devotee told me bluntly, "Women have a sisterhood bond and common maternal experience with Guadalupe that no man can replicate." In her work on the Guadalupan devotion of Mexican American women, theologian Jeanette Rodriguez illuminates the comfort, peace, and ability to sustain relationships Guadalupe embodies and inspires in women, as well as the strength Guadalupe gives them to endure difficulties and to do what needs to be done for their families, themselves, and their communities. Numerous women perceive Guadalupe as a model and supporter of their lives within and outside their homes, whether their efforts are aimed at struggling for safer neighborhoods, forming and nurturing their children in a complex world, insisting on moral standards in the community and its schools, having their husbands take on more responsibilities in child-rearing and household tasks, or pursuing meaningful work. Parish leader Esther Rodríguez from San Antonio, Texas attested, "Guadalupe gives you dignity to go places you haven't been before."

Finally, Guadalupe's countenance attracts her multitudes of devotees because they see someone whom they can trust and to whom they can freely pour out their hearts' concerns. Her litany of achievements, many of which her devotees call miracles, is endless: providing rain and abundant harvests, driving back flood waters, abating epidemics, safeguarding immigrants, protecting soldiers at war, restoring broken relationships, enabling students to have success in pursuing an education, providing help with employment, healing all manner of infirmity and distress. Prayers of petition and thanksgiving for her intercession flow continuously. In the hearts of her faithful followers, Guadalupe never fails. Turning to her is a surefire step in responding to a difficult or even hopeless situation. And what of the cancer patient who fails to recover, the son who shows no sign of turning from wrongful ways, the poverty that is endemic? What matters most to them is not that their prayers receive an answer in the manner they desire, but that they see in Guadalupe's face someone who cares about them, someone who is ever willing to listen.

In a word, what they see in Guadalupe's face is faithfulness, a mother, and a presence that never abandons them. Thus to look on the Guadalupe image is to encounter a celestial mother who embodies hope. As lay leader Socorro Durán from San Leandro, California put it, for people struggling with illness, poverty, unemployment, inadequate education, a lack of legal status, insecurity, or any kind of discouragement or difficulty, the Guadalupe image is a needed reminder that "a long time ago Our Lady's apparition to Juan Diego was a sudden, unexpected event which then and now brings hope and expectation to us, the descendants of Juan Diego."

References

Matovina, Timothy and Virgilio Elizondo. *The Treasure of Guadalupe.* Notre Dame, Indiana: University of Notre Dame Press, 2006.

PART VI

Specific
Populations

LITURGY FROM THE PERIPHERY:
A FARM WORKERS' LITURGY

Luis Beteta, MM

I t was seven years ago that someone spoke to me for the first time about the migrant community. It was useless to try to find the term *migrante* in a dictionary of the Spanish language; there was little printed material that could prepare me for an encounter with this group of people. It was thanks to the help of volunteers, during a summer Saturday or Sunday on the outskirts of Grand Rapids, Michigan, that I became acquainted with this booming, pious, cheerful, and hard-working community.

In some rural areas of the Diocese of Grand Rapids you are able to observe this scene: A bright afternoon when the parking lots of the local parishes begin to fill with cars and pickups, and generally no fewer than five people get out of each car, in some cases whole families in which one can identify the parents and the older children who jealously care for the littler ones.

In other cases, it isn't so easy to identify the relationship that unites those who come in the same car; a group of young people between the ages of 15 and 30 years, all male, slowly gets out dressed in jeans, with shiny metal belt buckles, cowboy boots, and cowboy hats, who respectfully remove their hats as they enter the temple. Their faces reflect the relief of the first hours of rest after an arduous week of work in the fields; hair just washed, clean clothes, and a smile on their face are common denominators.

Generally, at the door of the church are those who welcome them. In the faces of many migrants, together with that smile, there are also questioning eyes, searching for a friendly face. The reception of those who arrive is most important to the outcome of the liturgical celebration. To invite the celebrant community to enter and recognize the temple as their home will give them a sense of familiarity and, ideally, a temporary sense of belonging, because they know they are only pilgrims.

Perhaps they don't use the term *pilgrim*, but, for those who come to Michigan, their lives are a continual peregrination from Florida, Texas, or Mexico, and from here they will continue on to other states. This experience prepares them to be excellent citizens of a homeland that goes far beyond this world, and reflection on this fact is something one should have in mind while preparing a homily or catechesis.

This welcome has produced good fruit, as much for the migrant community as for those who have lived here for some time. Becoming conscious of this reality, it is important not to fall into paternalistic attitudes, because awakened eyes will be able to see that both groups are the object and subject of evangelization in their interaction and celebration that in the end are the same.

Familiarity with place on the part of the migrant community and the warm acceptance of the local community are much more visible when the temple reflects the religious experience of both groups, creating space within itself for the particular devotions of each one of the people that shares the place. On many occasions, one can observe the face of a worshiper searching for the Virgin of Guadalupe or the Virgin of San Juan of the Lakes, perhaps holding a candle in their hands without finding where to place it and leave there a burning testimony of the faith that inhabits his or her heart.

It is sad to observe that during these adaptations in the temple the local community does not engage in a discerning process, because what is unknown to them can also make them feel uncomfortable. Without a participative process to facilitate the harmonious encounter of both groups, the result can be counterproductive, and though people have made an attempt to reach something positive, misunderstandings and suspicions can arise.

In some cases, and with the objective of avoiding these situations, the image of the Virgin of Guadalupe comes out of the sacristy during the Spanish Mass, only to return there once the religious service is over. This situation creates a sense of insecurity and momentary tolerance, and in no way the sense of brotherly and sisterly reception and belonging to a place, which is very far from the spirit of the liturgy.

In many cases the presiding priest offers the welcome of the community as people enter the temple. Because of the burden of many pastoral tasks, generally he is not the same person each week and in many cases is not the pastor of the church. It is thanks to those dedicated priests that during the migrant season a sacramental accompaniment exists. When the priest who presides at Mass is the same during the whole season, and when he participates in the community beyond the liturgical celebrations, blending among the community in their daily life as he visits them in their homes, the domestic and ecclesial liturgy find a cumulative point in the Sunday Mass. Reaching this level of togetherness between the minister and the people is only possible when the minister doesn't have multiple communities under his pastoral care, as happens in most cases. This relationship nurtures stability for the migrant, and liturgical catechesis can unfold with greater clarity and in a progressive way.

In our diocese, one way we have attended to these needs has been through the presence of pastoral associates during the summer months. We designate pastoral associates, laymen, or laywomen with theological-pastoral formation who come from Mexico or other Latin American countries especially to give pastoral attention to the migrant community. Their work is closely coordinated with the local parishes and supported by the diocesan office seeking a *pastoral de conjunto.* This experience has had good results, because these people do not have the responsibilities of a local parish and can visit the migrants in their camps, share their happiness, listen to their experiences, and become a part of the community as much as possible.

I have listened to the rejoicing of more than one migrant as he or she mentions to the others that the priest who is "doing" the Mass, or the brother or sister who coordinates the Mass, was in their home the night before having supper with their family. In many cases, this familiarity with the minister creates such confidence that those who used to sit in the back during Mass were willing to participate in some liturgical ministry; and where a community only "observed" the sacrament, members of the community were later willing to take up the offering, proclaim the word, and be extraordinary ministers of Communion. In short, they took a more active part in the liturgy, thanks to pastoral accompaniment.

Having more time available to live among the migrants, pastoral associates also find themselves in a special situation that allows them to identify the leaders of the community, and also those who have academic preparation and possible vocations to priestly or religious life, making their accompaniment and spiritual development possible.

Permanent parishioners, even if they don't speak Spanish, make up a welcome committee. Having Hispanic residents of this or another parish accompany them undoubtedly facilitates spirit and warmth in the liturgy. It has also been helpful that someone with experience accompany so that, in dialogue with them, he or she will also be offering information and will help them to feel as if the migrant community is made up of people with not only equal rights but also equal obligations, such as participating in the liturgy.

I believe that music is one of the ministries requiring more support. Normally, volunteer Spanish speakers, mostly nearby residents of the area, make up the music ministry. Many people who have also participated in the music ministry in their own parishes are also overburdened, and it is not unusual that they haven't been able to take enough time for their families. In many cases, they are the only ones who sing the song while the rest of the community just looks on, either because they don't know the hymns or because the hymns aren't appealing.

I have known occasions, during a song with a *ranchera* rhythm, when the song not only drew the attention of the community but also inspired the people to sing energetically, even ad-libbing the words and clapping their hands. During these moments one does not hear the noise of children and babies, as happens during the homily or the rest of the liturgy, because the music also captivates the littlest ones.

Although achieving the participation of many migrants in music ministry hasn't been an easy task, it is not unusual to see young people with musical aptitude who don't even possess the instrument that they know how to play, because it is difficult for them to move from place to place without damaging it. I have seen a great number of people willing to participate when musical instruments are available for their use, and when the local group or choir is willing to coordinate and include them in the ministry.

Regarding the Liturgy of the Word and reflecting upon it, it is evident that when reflection on the word is tied to daily life, it definitely penetrates with greater depth the minds and hearts of the community. This result is indubitable as we observe the people and chat with them after a Mass that a minister who lives and understands the world of a migrant has celebrated.

When liturgical celebrations somehow incorporate agricultural products, either in the procession, in the liturgical setting of the worship space, or in the presentation of the gifts, the community acquires a deeper sense of participation, be it in the celebration of Mass in the parish or in migrant camps.

During Communion, on more than one occasion, I have seen that basic knowledge, such as when to respond "Amen," is lacking. This lack of basic knowledge is a consequence of the rupture of the system of family life through which faith and knowledge about it are transmitted in their culture. The grandmothers, first educators of the faith, are not part of daily life, and the function of formation of the child on the part of the extended family has been replaced. This problem exemplifies only the tip of the iceberg. Due to the breaking off of relationships with an extended family occurring in their place of origin, moral and social values have been fractured. I believe it is very important to keep this fact in mind when planning the content of what is to be transmitted in Sunday school, during all catechesis, and in the liturgy.

Unfortunately, the lack of time to dialogue with the people and the desire to serve the community cause other elements to be included in the celebration of the Eucharist: messages about social, medical, and religious services. Something similar happens in the celebration of some *quinceañeras* and weddings, which because of extenuating circumstances are celebrated during Sunday Mass, something that detaches the community from the liturgical spirituality of Sunday.

In one of our parishes, women, not all of whom speak Spanish or are of Hispanic ethnic origin, have formed a group. After the Mass, they offer coffee and doughnuts, creating an atmosphere conducive to fellowship; the migrant community receives this warmth and sincerity with much appreciation. To have a group like this is very useful for building bridges between the migrant and resident communities, making them most faithful defenders in time of need.

At the end of the Mass, a cordial greeting from the minister has been common in our liturgies. Together with this pleasant greeting I will always remember the last Mass of the migrant season I observed seven years ago. Cars drew near to door of the church. It was October and the days were getting shorter. The night was very dark, and the cars passed in front of the priest who blessed them, and then they continued on their pilgrimage. A few possessions—a truck, the family, and their faith to illumine the way—were their whole "knapsack," and they stirred up in my memory the children of Israel marching toward the promised land.

Seven years have passed, and today, clearer than ever, I am conscious that they are a contradiction to our consumer society. They are the ones who minister and they are the ones who fill our parishes with blessings of their passing presence.

From ¡Gracias! Magazine, May/June 2002, previously published six times a year by Liturgy Training Publications of the Archdiocese of Chicago.

_____ *Luis Beteta,* MM

HISPANIC YOUTH:
EVANGELIZERS AND MESSENGERS OF HOPE
THROUGH LITURGICAL CELEBRATIONS

Sr. Angela Erevia, MCDP

In *The Hispanic Presence: Challenge and Commitment—A Pastoral Letter on Hispanic Ministry* (1983), the Catholic bishops of the United States expressed their deepest sentiments about the Hispanic presence in the United States of America: "At this moment of grace we recognize the Hispanic community among us a blessing from God. We call upon all persons of good faith to share our vision of the special gifts which Hispanics bring to the Body of Christ, His Pilgrim Church on earth (1 Cor. 12:12–13)" (no. 1). This document also called for a convocation of the *III Encuentro*: "We ask our Hispanic people to raise their prophetic voices to us once again, as they did in 1972 and 1977, in a *III Encuentro Nacional Hispano de Pastoral*, so that together we can face our responsibilities well. We call for the launching of an *Encuentro* process, to dioceses and regions, and to the national level, culminating in a gathering of representatives in Washington, D.C. in August 1985" (no. 18).

An intense process at the diocesan and regional levels began in preparation for the national gathering. The *III Encuentro Nacional Hispano de Pastoral* convened with over 1,200 delegates in attendance. The Church once again heard the voices of the people, and the results were published in *Prophetic Voices*. Five statements of commitment dealt with evangelization, integral education, social justice, youth, and leadership formation. It was significant that the conclusions included a section on youth as a major component.

In both of the previous documents, the Catholic bishops acknowledged the Christian values of the Hispanic family:

> Among these are: profound respect for the dignity of each *person*, reflecting the example of Christ in the gospels; deep and reverential love for *family life*, where the entire extended family discovers its roots, its identity, and its strength; a marvelous sense of *community* that celebrates life through "fiesta"; loving appreciation for God's gift of *life*, and an understanding of time which allows one to savor that gift; and authentic and consistent devotion to Mary, the Mother of God (no. 3).

One treasured gift of the Hispanic family is their sons and daughters. A strong and firm belief in God—*la Providencia*—shapes and nurtures their faith. The use of many expressions of God strengthens it as well: *Primero Dios. En el nombre sea de Dios. Buenos días le dé Dios. Que Dios te bendiga. Vaya con Dios. Si Dios quiere. Si Dios nos da licencia. Si Dios nos presta vida y salud.* Family beliefs, gospel values, cultural traditions, and religious celebrations play a big role in the way young people learn and live their faith.

Pope John Paul II greatly understood and appreciated young people. Concurrent with the United Nations' proclamation of the International Youth Year, John Paul II invited young people for a meeting with him in Rome: "1985 was the International Youth Year proclaimed by the United Nations, and 300,000 young people had a meeting with the Pope in Saint Peter's Square on Palm Sunday. . . . In December of that year, Pope John Paul II announced that there would be an annual World Youth Day beginning on the next Palm Sunday" (Pontifical Council for the Laity). World Youth Day would be held every year at the diocesan level. From 1987, with an interval of two or three years, world gatherings of young people were held with the Holy Father in a different country each time.

John Paul II was very demonstrative in expressing his love and compassion for young people. He initiated World Youth Day as a sign of his unwavering faith in them and as a testimony to their natural goodness. He demonstrated great confidence in them and in their generosity and ability to respond to Christ. At the same time he challenged them, and he affirmed their potential to be true disciples of Jesus. He created the pilgrimage of the youth cross as part of World Youth Days. "It was the Holy Year of Redemption (1983-1984). Pope John Paul II felt that there should be a cross—the symbol of our faith—near the main altar in Saint Peter's Basilica where it could be seen by everyone. A large wooden Cross, 3.8 metres high, was placed there according to the Holy Father's desire" (Pontifical Council for the Laity).

At the end of the Holy Year, after the pope had closed the Holy Door, he entrusted that cross to the youth of the world, whom the young people from San Lorenzo Youth Centre in Rome represented. His words on that occasion were: "My dear young people, at the conclusion of this Holy Year, I entrust to you the sign of this Jubilee Year: the Cross of Christ! Carry it throughout the world as a symbol of Christ's love for humanity, and announce to everyone that only

_____ *Sr. Angela Erevia, MCDP*

in the death and resurrection of Christ can we find salvation and redemption" (Pontifical Council for the Laity).

The pope's message to the youth of the world certainly resonates with Hispanic young people of our own faith communities. When family and community mean so much to them, the decision to leave family and friends behind has placed them in the shadow of the cross. Sustained by an indomitable faith in Christ, the suffering Christ, they pursue their dreams for a better life for themselves and their families. In their own personal experience of suffering, they experience the suffering of Christ. They recount incredible stories about their dangerous journeys from their countries of origin into this country. The symbol of the cross has been, is, and will be the banner they hold up before them in their daily struggles. The Catholic Church in the United States is truly blessed with the vibrant, youthful presence of thousands of Hispanic young people. They constitute a powerful source of energy, talent, service, and commitment to the gospel of Jesus Christ. This fact was very evident at the first national gathering of Hispanic youth at the University of Notre Dame.

The *Primer Encuentro Nacional de Pastoral Juvenil Hispana* was held at the University of Notre Dame in South Bend, Indiana in June, 2006. Its theme was "*Tejiendo el Futuro Juntos*—Weaving the Future Together." It was a magnificent celebration filled with tremendous joy, energy, and hope for the Catholic Church in the United States. It was the culmination of a long journey taken by thousands of Hispanic youth who affirmed their faith in the Lord Jesus. More than two thousand young delegates represented 129 dioceses at this historic event. They visibly and enthusiastically demonstrated that the Catholic Church is very much alive and well in the various regions of the nation. The gathering at Notre Dame, preceded by many months of planning, was a dream comes true for Hispanic youth leaders.

> The central goal of the *First Encuentro* was to engage Hispanic young people and the professional leadership in Hispanic and youth and young adult ministry in a process of encounter-conversion-communion-solidarity and mission that can empower Hispanic young people into a more active, enthusiastic, and influential participation in the life and mission of the Church in the United States (from the *Encuentro Manual*).

Hispanic Youth Liturgical Celebrations ———————————————**119**

The consultation process in preparation for the First National Encuentro happened at three levels: parish, diocesan, and regional. Parish, diocesan, and regional leaders of *la pastoral juvenil* facilitated each process. It was an intense and thorough process that created a forum for the voice of youth and young adults to be heard. Five significant themes were discussed—encountering the living Jesus Christ, the path to conversion, the path to communion, the path to solidarity, and Jesus calls us to be missionaries—and the responses were recorded for further reflection and sharing at the First National Encuentro.

After a lengthy journey of very productive and inspiring parish, diocesan, and regional *encuentros*, we gathered at Notre Dame, not as strangers but as brothers and sisters to celebrate our cultural roots and our Catholic faith. With the exchange of *abrazos* by the delegates, it was evident that this was going to be a faith-filled experience. A deep sense of gratitude for the faith and spirituality Hispanic youth displayed inspired all youth leaders who witnessed those encounters. All during the event the young people demonstrated great love and respect for one another, tremendous reverence at prayer, great sharing at meal times, a great desire to learn and to process what was being presented, and a great capacity to celebrate God's goodness in their lives.

Today, Hispanic youth are asking the same question the young man who approached Jesus did: "Good Teacher, what must I do to receive eternal life?" (Mark 10:17). They have an inner profound desire for holiness. Their insatiable hunger and thirst for a deeper knowledge, understanding, and appreciation of God in their lives is quite evident from their numerous responses. They are not afraid to make a commitment to serve the Lord. They have expressed an earnest desire to study *la Palabra*. One area of church life in which they have demonstrated great creativity is the liturgy.

By participating in the liturgical life of the Church, Hispanic youth exercise their baptismal right to celebrate liturgy in its widest sense. The *Catechism of the Catholic Church* states, "The word 'liturgy' originally meant a 'public work' or a 'service in the name of/on behalf of the people.' In Christian tradition it means the participation of the People of God in 'the work of God' . . ." (no. 1069). "In the New Testament the word 'liturgy' refers not only to the celebration of divine worship but also to the proclamation of the gospel and to active charity" (no. 1070).

And from the *Constitution on the Sacred Liturgy*: "In liturgical celebrations each one, minister or layperson, who has an office to perform, should do all of, but only, those parts which pertain to that office by the nature of the rite and the principles of liturgy" (no. 28). "Servers, lectors, commentators, and members of the choir also exercise a genuine liturgical function. They ought to discharge their office, therefore, with the sincere devotion and decorum demanded by so exalted a ministry and rightly expected of them by God's people" (no. 29). Later on, when other ministries were recognized, "such as extraordinary ministers of Holy Communion, ministers to the sick, ministers of hospitality, liturgy became again a work of the people. The community took ownership of their prayer" (Pérez, 378).

This description of liturgy provides a wide range of opportunities for young people to be actively involved in God's work. They are already making significant contributions to the body of Christ at different levels and in varying degrees of service. They are actively engaged in the life of the Church in their respective parishes as catechists, ministers of hospitality, lectors, commentators, extraordinary ministers of Holy Communion, altar servers, and choir leaders. They trust generous adults who create opportunities for them to exercise their God-given gifts and talents.

The Church is blessed to claim so many adults who are so generous and willing to minister to the young people. In the *Decree on the Apostolate of the Laity*, the bishops at Vatican II stated the important role adults play in the lives of youth: "Adults ought to engage in friendly discussion with young people so that both groups, overcoming the age barrier, can become acquainted and can share the special benefits each generation has to offer the other. Adults should attract young persons to the apostolate first by good example, and, if the opportunity presents itself, by offering them balanced advice and effective assistance" (no. 12). Adult mentors can accompany Hispanic young people and model for them how to live healthy, holy, and happy lives. These mentors help to sustain and nurture Hispanic youth to be active in the life of the Church. Following the example of John Paul II, these adults develop leadership from among the youth by involving them in planning creative activities around the liturgical calendar of the Church.

Our Lady of Guadalupe

For hundreds of years the feast of Our Lady of Guadalupe, celebrated on December 12, has provided and will provide in the future an excellent opportunity for evangelization. Some parishes offer families the opportunity to host a day of the novena in preparation for the feast. Annual public celebrations take place in churches, cathedrals, assembly halls, and public arenas around the country to honor the Mother of God.

Young people have been very resourceful in dramatizing the dialogue between Our Lady and Juan Diego. Our Lady, tenderly calling him by name, invited Juan Diego to be her special messenger of hope for a suffering people. Juan Diego felt unworthy to be Our Lady's messenger. Many young people can identify with him. They feel unworthy to be so involved in the life of the Church. They need to hear the words of love and assurance Mary spoke to Juan Diego: "Am I not here, I, who am your mother? Are you not under my shadow and protection? Am I not the source of your joy? Are you not in the hollow of my mantle, in the crossing of my arms? Do you need something more?" (*Nican Mopohua*). They can be the evangelizers and the messengers of hope for other young people who like them are struggling to live healthy and holy lives.

Las Posadas

Hispanics prepare for the celebration of Christmas in a special way by enacting the journey of Mary and Joseph to Bethlehem: *Las Posadas*. For nine days, families participate in *Las Posadas* in neighborhood, parish, and other settings. Young people can lead them in prayer each day by announcing a particular theme, followed by a brief introduction, dramatizing a selected scriptural reading (biblical text in parentheses below), and allowing time for personal reflection in the format of *lectio divina*. People can celebrate this form of prayer before the traditional *Posadas* or when bad weather prevents them from going outside.

• Day 1: Search. We search for the meaning of our lives. We search for the will of God for us. We search for love, friendship, happiness, and for others to respect us. We search to be faithful sons and daughters of God (Luke 2:1–7, Joseph and Mary look for shelter in Bethlehem; Luke 2:8ff, shepherds look for the Infant Jesus; Matthew 2:1ff, the magi look for the infant Jesus; Luke 2:41–52, Joseph and Mary look for Jesus; Matthew 18:10–14, the good shepherd looks for lost sheep; John 3:1–21, Nicodemus looks for God's kingdom).

• Day 2: Pilgrimage. We are a pilgrim church. We are pilgrims and companions on our faith journey. We believe that God walks with us to sustain, protect, and heal us. We walk with the assurance that God is with us and that Jesus is the way, the truth, and the life (John 14:6).

• Day 3: Encounter. On our faith journey, we meet many persons—members of our family, members of our faith community, people we work with. We respect the dignity of each person because we are all created in the image of God. We are sons and daughters of the same Father and brothers and sisters to one another (John 4:4ff, the Samaritan woman meets Jesus; John 20:11ff, Mary Magdalene meets Jesus).

• Day 4: The right to be born. Life is a gift of God to us. We had the right to be born according to God's plan. Many children have been denied that right due to abortion. We pray to God for all mothers who have had an abortion. We ask the Lord to comfort them (Luke 2:4–7, Jesus is born in Bethlehem).

• Day 5: The poor. The poor are those persons among us who do not have control over their own time. They depend on the kindness of others for what they need. A strong and firm faith in God sustains the poor. They reflect the face of God in the world. Jesus tells us that what we do to the poor, we do to him. Jesus also praised the poor widow for her generosity (Matthew 25:31–46, the final judgment; Luke 21:1–4, a widow gives from her poverty).

• Day 6: The stranger. All human beings are created in the image of God. We are the sons and daughters of the one Father. We are brothers and sisters to one another. Strangers are those persons whom we do not know. We also become strangers when we do not treat others with respect. As brothers and sisters, we welcome others to our faith communities. Jesus identifies himself with the stranger (Matthew 2:13–15, the escape to Egypt; Matthew 25:35).

• Day 7: Hospitality. *Hospes*, an old English word with Greek roots, means "healing love." "Hospitality" is derived from this word. When we welcome others, we offer them the healing love of God. Jesus gave us the example of welcoming others by the way he treated the widow, the orphan, the stranger, the sinner. When we welcome others, we welcome Jesus himself (1 John 4:7–21, God is love; John

13:l–15, Jesus washes the feet of the apostles; Matthew 25:35-36).

• Day 8: Light. Jesus is the Light of the world. He invites us to be a light in the world for one another in our families, communities, and places of work. He invites us to lessen evil in the world. Light represents the good in the world, while darkness represents evil and sin. Jesus invites us to be a light for one another (John 8:12, Jesus, the light of the world; Matthew 5:14–16, Jesus invites us to be a light).

• Day 9: Fiesta. The birth of Jesus calls for a fiesta. We celebrate the birth of Jesus: the Son of God and the Son of Mary. The Son of God became human to show us God's unconditional love. By celebrating Jesus' birth, we celebrate our own gift of life.

On the last day of *Las Posadas,* an image of the Child Jesus is placed in the crib before the celebration of Midnight Mass.

Pasión de Cristo

The Passion of Jesus on Good Friday has great meaning for young people. They prayerfully and reverently enact events in the Passion of Christ, including the Last Supper; the Agony in the Garden; the arrest of Jesus; Jesus before the Sanhedrin; Peter's denial of Jesus; the soldiers beating Jesus; Jesus before Pilate; Jesus before Herod; Jesus returning to Pilate, who condemns him to die; and the release of Barabbas. The way of the cross continues through the streets of the city or the surrounding area. Invited to carry the cross between stations are fathers, mothers, the single, widowed, divorced and/or separated, priests and religious, persons having someone in prison, women who had an abortion or lost a child, the elderly, youth, and children. The way of the cross ends with the Crucifixion, the Seven Last Words of Jesus on the cross, his death, and Jesus taken down from the cross and placed in his tomb.

On Palm Sunday, the beginning of Holy Week, the young people enacting the Passion gather for a retreat. They prepare the environment with symbols of the Passion. All of those having a part to play are asked beforehand to be prepared to share how they feel about the role assigned to them. The main characters are Jesus, Mary, Peter, John, James, Judas, the rest of the apostles, Pilate, Herod, Caiaphas, Barabbas, the soldiers, Simon of Cyrene, the holy women of Jerusalem, and the centurion. Their faith-sharing is a powerful testimony of the depth of their spirituality and commitment to the Lord.

Nocturnal adoration before the Blessed Sacrament

Nocturnal adoration attracts young people. They take turns spending the night on their knees with extended arms before the Blessed Sacrament. They identify with the suffering Christ to the extent of wanting to accompany the Lord in his sufferings. They value spending time before the presence of Jesus in the Blessed Sacrament. They have chosen to spend time in prayer instead of placing themselves in harmful situations.

Mother's Day

On Mother's Day young people give special tribute to mothers by going from house to house in the early hours of the morning serenading them. At Mass mothers are honored with a priest's blessing, while the youth present them with a rose to thank them for the gift of life. A fiesta may follow in their honor after Mass.

Special blessings

As young people graduate, many go away to college or join the military. For some it is their first time away from home. At a family gathering, parents bless them, asking God to protect and to keep them safe from all dangers. A Christian symbol—a crucifix, a medal, a holy card—is given to them as a reminder that they are not alone on their journey through life.

References

Pérez, Arturo J. In *Hispanic Catholic Culture in the U.S.: Issues and Concerns*, Jay P. Dolan and Allan Figueroa Deck, eds. Notre Dame, Indiana: University of Notre Dame Press, 1994.

Pontifical Council for the Laity. "The road to Cologne." Rome: July 2003.

National Conference of Catholic Bishops. *Prophetic Voices: The Document on the Process of the III Encuentro Nacional Hispano de Pastoral*. Washington, DC: NCCB, 1986.

National Conference of Catholic Bishops. *The Hispanic Presence: Challenge and Commitment: A Pastoral Letter on Hispanic Ministry*. Washington, DC: NCCB, 1983.

BILINGUAL
LITURGICAL VOCABULARY
SPANISH-ENGLISH

A

abad: abbot
abadía: abbey
absolución: absolution
abstenerse: to abstain
acetre: aspersorium
  (holy water bucket)
ácimo, ázimo: unleavened bread
acólitos: acolytes
adoración: adoration
adorar: to worship
adviento: Advent
agua bautismal: baptismal water
agua bendita: holy water
ahijada: goddaughter
ahijado: godson
alba: alb
altar: altar
ambón: ambo
amito: amice
anillo: ring
**anotación del bautismo
administrado, fe de bautismo:**
  notation of baptism
apóstol: apostle
archiabad: archabbot
arquidiócesis: archdiocese
arras: wedding coins
arrodillarse, de rodillas: to
  kneel
arzobispo: archbishop
ataúd: coffin, casket
atrio: vestibule, porch
aureola: halo
ayuno: fast

B

báculo: crosier, staff
bajo condición: conditional
banco: pew
banquete pascual: Passover
baptisterio: baptistery
bautismo por infusión: baptism
  by infusion
bautismo por inmersión:
  baptism by immersion
bautizar: to baptize, to christen
bendecir: to bless
bendición: blessing
biblia: Bible
blasfemia: blasphemy
boda: wedding

C

cáliz: chalice
campana: bell
campanario: bell tower, steeple
capa pluvial: cope
capellán: chaplain
capilla: chapel
**carácter sacramental (sello
espiritual indeleble):**
  sacramental character
cardenal: cardinal (eccl.)
caso de necesidad: case of
  necessity
casulla: chasuble
cátedra: cathedra (priest's chair)
catedral: cathedral
catequesis: catechesis
cementerio: cemetery

ceniza, miércoles de:
  Ash Wednesday
chambelán de honor: best man
cielo: heaven
cima: summit
cíngulo: cincture
cirio pascual: paschal candle
clérigo: cleric, clergyman
clero: the clergy
coche fúnebre: hearse
cojines: cushions (matrimony)
colecta: collection
comulgante: communicant
comulgar: to receive
  Communion
concupiscencia (inclinación
  al pecado): concupiscence
  (inclination to sin)
confesión: confession
confeti: confetti
confirmación: confirmation
consagrar: to consecrate
copón: ciborium
coro: choir
corporal: corporal
cota: rochet, short-sleeved
  surplice
crisma (óleo perfumado y
consagrado por el obispo):
  chrism
crucifijo: crucifix
cruz: cross
cruz pectoral: pectoral cross
cuaresma: Lent
culto: cult, rite
culto de la eucaristía:
  eucharistic worship
custodia: monstrance

D
dama de honor: bridesmaid
desarrollo de la fe: development
  of the faith
diácono: deacon
diezmo: tithe, tithing
difunto, finado: deceased
diócesis (la): diocese
duda sobre la validez del
bautismo: doubt about the
  validity of baptism

E
entierro: burial
entredicho: interdict
Epifanía: Epiphany
escapulario: scapular
estatua: statue
estipendio: stipend
estola: stole
etapas (pasos sucesivos): stages
eucaristía: Eucharist
evangeliario: Gospel book
examen de conciencia:
  examination of conscience
excolmulgado: excommunicated
exequias: funeral rites
exorcismo: exorcism
exposición del Santísimo
  Sacramento: Exposition of the
  Blessed Sacrament

F
fiel: faithful
fieles (los): congregation
fiestas de guardar: holy days of
  obligation
fracción del pan: breaking of
  bread
fuente bautismal: baptismal font
funeral: funeral

G

gaudete, domingo de: Gaudete Sunday

golpes de pecho se reza el "Yo confieso": to strike one's breast when reciting "I confess"

H

hábito: habit (religious)
hijo adoptivo: adopted child
hisopo: aspergillum
homilía: homily
hostia: host
humeral: humeral veil

I

ícono: icon
iglesia parroquial: parish church
incensario: thurible
incienso: incense
incineración: cremation
incruenta: unbloody
infierno: hell
iniciación cristiana: Christian initiation

J

juramento: oath

L

laico: lay
lamentarse: to mourn
lámpara del sagrario: sanctuary lamp
lápida: tombstone
lavabo: washbasin
lazo: lazo (wedding custom)
lazos de caridad: bonds of charity

lazos desordenados: inordinate attachments
leccionario: Lectionary
lectura: reading
letanía: litany
libro de bautismos: baptismal register
lícitamente: licitly, legitimately
liturgia: liturgy

LL

llave del sagrario: tabernacle key

M

madrina: sponsor (female)
manera no cruenta: unbloody manner
mantel del altar: altarcloth
mantilla: mantilla (made of lace)
matrimonio: marriage
mausoleo: mausoleum
ministro: minister
ministro extraordinario de la santa comunión: extraordinary minister of Holy Communion
misa: Mass
misal: missal
misterio: mystery
mitra: miter
monaguillo/a: altar server
monasterio: monastery
monja: nun
monje: monk
monseñor: bishop (Latin America)

N

nave: nave
nave lateral: aisle
nochebuena: Christmas Eve
novenario: novena
nueva alianza: new covenant

O

obispado: bishop's residence
obispo: bishop
ofertorio: offertory
óleo de los catecúmenos: oil of catechumens
órdenes sagradas: holy orders
ordinario del lugar (obispo diocesano): ordinary

P

padre: father (priest)
padrino: godfather, sponsor (male)
pagano: heathen, pagan
palia: pall, altar cloth
palio: pallium, cloak
pan ácimo, ázimo: unleavened bread
papa (el): pope
párroco: pastor
parroquia: parish
patena: paten
paternidad: paternity
pecado: sin
pecado grave: grave, serious sin
pecado original: original sin
penitencia: penance
pila bautismal: baptismal font
píxide: pyx
plegaria eucarística: Eucharistic Prayer

prédica: sermon
predicar: to preach
prefacio: Preface
presbiterio: presbytery
presbítero: priest
presencia eucarística: eucharistic presence
presencia real: Real Presence
promesas solemnes: solemn vows
púlpito: pulpit
purificador: purificator

R

reclinatorio: kneeler
reconciliación: reconciliation
religioso/a: religious
reliquia: relic
renovación de las promesas del bautismo: renewal of baptismal promises
retablo: altarpiece, retable
rezar: to pray
rito: rite
ritual: ritual
roquete: rochet
rosario: rosary
rúbrica: rubric

S

sacerdote, cura: priest
sacramentario: Sacramentary
sacramentos: sacraments
sacrificio cruento: bloody sacrifice
sacristán: sacristan
sagrario: tabernacle
salmo: psalm
Santa Sede: Holy See

santísimo sacramento: Blessed
Sacrament
semana santa: Holy Week
seminarista: seminarian
señal de la cruz: sign of the
cross
sermón: sermon
sobrepelliz: surplice
solideo: zuchetto
sotana: cassock

T
tabernáculo: tabernacle
templo del Espíritu Santo:
temple of the Holy Spirit
testigo de bautismo: baptismal
witness
triduo pascual: Easter Triduum,
Paschal Triduum
turíbelo: thurible

U
última cena: Last Supper
unción: anointing

V
vela: candle
velorio: wake
vestidura blanca: white
vestment, garment
vestiduras: vestments
vestuario litúrgico: sacred
vestments
via crucis: way of the cross,
stations of the cross
viático: viaticum
vicario parroquial: associate
pastor, parochial vicar
víctima: victim

vigilia pascual: Paschal Vigil
villancico: carol
vinajeras: cruets
vínculo sacramental de unidad:
sacramental bond of unity
visita al santísimo sacramento:
visit to the Blessed Sacrament

ENGLISH-SPANISH

A
abbey: abadía
abbot: abad
absolution: absolución
(to) abstain: abstenerse
acolytes: acólitos
adopted child: hijo adoptivo
adoration: adoración
Advent: adviento
aisle: nave lateral, ala, costado
alb: alba
altar: altar
altar cloth: mantel
altar server: monaguillo (m.),
monaguilla (f.)
ambo: ambón
amice: amito
anointing: unción
apostle: apóstol
archabbot: archiabad
archbishop: arzobispo
archdiocese: arquidiócesis
Ash Wednesday: miércoles
de ceniza
aspergillum: hisopo
aspersorium (holy water
bucket): acetre
associate pastor, parochial
pastor: vicario parroquial

B

baptism by immersion: bautismo por inmersión
baptism by infusion: bautismo por infusión
baptismal font: pila bautismal
baptismal register: libro de bautismo
baptismal water: agua bautismal
baptismal witness: testigo de bautismo
baptistery: baptisterio
(to) baptize, (to) christen: bautizar
bell: campana
bell tower, steeple: campanario
best man: chambelán
Bible: biblia
bishop: obispo, monseñor (Latin America)
bishop's residence: obispado
blasphemy: blasfemia
(to) bless: bendecir
blessing: bendición
bloody sacrifice: sacrificio cruento
bonds of charity: lazos de caridad
breaking of bread: fracción del pan
bridesmaid: dama de honor

C

candle: candela, vela
cardinal (eccl.): cardenal
carol: villancico
case of necessity: caso de necesidad
cassock: sotana

catechesis: catequesis
cathedra (priest's chair): cátedra
cathedral: catedral
cemetery: cementerio, camposanto
chalice: cáliz
chapel: capilla
chaplain: capellán
chasuble: casulla
choir: coro
chrism: crisma
Christian initiation: iniciación cristiana
ciborium: copón
cincture: cíngulo
clergy: el clero
cleric, clergyman: clérigo
coffin: féretro, ataúd
collection: limosna
communicant: comulgante
concupiscence (inclination to sin): concupiscencia (inclinación al pecado)
confession: confesión
confetti: confetti
confirmation: confirmación
congregation: congregación, los fieles
(to) consecrate: consagrar
cope: capa pluvial
corporal: corporal
cremation: incineración
crosier, staff: báculo
crucifix: crucifijo
cruets: vinajeras
cult, rite: culto, rito
cushions (wedding): cojines

D

deacon: diácono
deceased: finado, difunto, fallecido
development of the faith:
    desarrollo de la fe
diocese: diócesis
doubt about the validity of
baptism: duda sobre la validez
    del bautismo

E

Epiphany: Epifanía
Eucharist: Eucaristía
Eucharistic Prayer: oración o
    plegaria eucarística
eucharistic presence: presencia
    eucarística
eucharistic worship: adoración
    eucarística
examination of conscience:
    examen de conciencia
excommunicated: excomulgado
exorcism: exorcismo
Exposition of the Blessed
    Sacrament: Exposición del
    Santísimo Sacramento
extraordinary minister of
    Holy Communion: ministro
    extraordinario de la santa
    comunión

F

fast: ayuno
father: padre (sacerdote)
funeral: funeral
funeral rites: exequias

G

Gaudete Sunday: domingo de
    gaudete

goddaughter: ahijada
godfather: padrino
godmother: madrina
godson: ahijado
grave, serious sin: pecado grave

H

habit (religious): hábito
halo: aureola
hearse: coche fúnebre
hell: infierno
holy days of obligation: fiestas
    de precepto, fiestas de guardar
Holy See: Santa Sede (Vaticano)
holy water: agua bendita
Holy Week: semana santa
homily: homilía
host: hostia
humeral veil: humeral

I

icon: ícono
incense: incienso
inordinate attachments: lazos
    desordenados

K

(to) kneel: arrodillarse
kneeler: reclinatorio

L

Last Supper: la última cena
lay: laico
lazo (wedding): lazo
Lectionary: leccionario
Lent: cuaresma
licitly, legitimately:
    legitimamente, lícito
litany: letanía
liturgy: liturgia

M

mantilla (made of lace): mantilla
marriage: boda, matrimonio
Mass: misa
mausoleum: mausoleo
minister: ministro
monk: monje
monstrance: custodia
(to) mourn: lamentarse

N

nave: nave
new covenant: nueva alianza
notation of baptism: anotación
del bautismo administrado,
fe de bautismo
novena: novena, novenario
nun: monja

O

oath: juramento
offertory: ofertorio
oil of catechumens: óleo de los
catecúmenos
ordinary: ordinario
original sin: pecado original

P

pall: palia
pallium: palio
parish: parroquia
parish church: iglesia parroquial
parishioners: parroquianos
paschal candle: cirio pascual
Paschal Vigil: vigilia pascual
Passover: la pascua
pastor: pastor
paten: patena
paternity: paternidad
pectoral cross: cruz pectoral

penance: penitencia
pew: banco
pope: el papa
(to) pray: orar, rezar
Preface: prefacio
presbytery: presbiterio
priest: sacerdote, cura, padre
pulpit: púlpito
purificator: purificador
pyx: píxide

R

Real Presence: presencia real
(to) receive Communion: recibir
comunión
reconciliation: reconciliación
rectory: casa cural, rectoría
relic: reliquia
religious: religioso (m.),
religiosa (f.)
renewal of baptismal promises:
enovación de las promesas
bautismales
ring: anillo
rite: rito
ritual: ritual
rochet: roquete
rosary: rosario
rubric: rúbrica

S

sacramental bond of unity: lazo
de unión sacramental
sacramental character: carácter
sacramental
Sacramentary: sacramentario
sacraments: sacramentos
sacred vestments: vestimenta
sagrada

sacristan: sacristán
sanctuary lamp: lámpara del
  sagrario
scapular: escapulario
seminarian: seminarista
sermon: sermón, prédica
sign of the cross: signo de la
  cruz, señal de la cruz
sin: pecado
solemn vows: votos solemnes
sponsors: padrinos, padrino
  (masc.), madrina (fem.)
stages: etapas
statue: estatua
stipend: estipendio
stole: estola
(to) strike one's chest when
  reciting "I confess": darse
  golpes de pecho al rezar
  "Yo confieso"
summit: cima
surplice: sobrepelliz

T
tabernacle: tabernáculo, sagrario
tabernacle key: llave del sagrario
temple of the Holy Spirit:
  templo del Espíritu Santo
thurible: turíbulo, incensario
tithe, tithing: diezmo, dar el
  diezmo
tombstone: lápida

U
unbloody manner: manera no
  cruenta
unleavened bread: pan ácimo,
  ázimo

V
vestments: vestimenta
viaticum: viático
victim: víctima
visit to the Blessed Sacrament:
  visita al santísimo sacramento
  del altar

W
wake: velorio
washbasin: lavabo
way of the cross, stations of the
  cross: vía crucis
wedding: boda
wedding coins: arras
white vestment, garment:
  vestidura blanca
(to) worship: adorar

Z
zucchetto: solideo

CONTRIBUTORS

Luis Beteta, M.M., is married and the father of two children. For the past twelve years he has been Director of Hispanic Ministry for the Diocese of Grand Rapids. He has a background of studies in theology and philosophy, a bachelor's degree with a major in pedagogy and minors in Spanish language and literature, and a master's degree in management. He is teaching courses related to cultural awareness at Grand Valley State University, and until June 2006 was chair of the Midwest Regional Association of Hispanic Ministry.

Peter J. Casarella, associate professor of systematic theology, The Catholic University of America, is the coeditor of *Cuerpo de Cristo: The Hispanic Presence in the U.S. Catholic Church*. He served from 2005–2006 as president of the Academy of Catholic Hispanic Theologians of the United States (ACHTUS).

Kenneth G. Davis, OFM **Conv.**, is a Conventual Franciscan teaching at the Saint Meinrad School of Theology in Indiana. For more information, see his Web site: http://kennethgdavis.com.

Sister Angela Erevia, MCDP, is a member of the Missionary Catechists of Divine Providence based in San Antonio, Texas. She has a master of religious education degree from the University of St. Thomas in Houston, Texas. She has served the Church for over fifty years in various positions at the parish, diocesan, state, regional, and national levels, including some United States Conference of Catholic Bishops committees. Presently she serves on the board of directors of the USCCB Commission on Certification and Accreditation. She is the author of many articles on the tradition of celebrating a young person's fifteenth birthday, including a bilingual book, *Quince Años: Celebrando la Vida Celebrating Life*. She is a member of the Catholic Faith Formation Office as the coordinator of Hispanic Ministry for the Archdiocese of Omaha.

Sister Rosa María Icaza, CCVI, Ph.D., is a Sister of Charity of the Incarnate Word and a member of the pastoral team at the Mexican American Cultural Center, San Antonio, Texas. She is a member of the

Subcommittee on Hispanic Liturgy of the U.S. Bishops' Committee on the Liturgy and a member of the Instituto Nacional Hispano de Liturgia.

Timothy Matovina, Ph.D. is associate professor of theology and the William and Anna Jean Cushwa Director of the Cushwa Center for the Study of American Catholicism at the University of Notre Dame. His most recent books are *Guadalupe and Her Faithful: Latino Catholics in San Antonio, from Colonial Origins to the Present* (2005) and, with Virgilio Elizondo and Allan Figueroa Deck, *The Treasure of Guadalupe* (2006).

Nury Nuila-Stevens, a native of El Salvador, received her master of arts degree from the University of Louisville, Kentucky. Currently she teaches Spanish at Saint Meinrad School of Theology in Indiana.

Bishop Ricardo Ramírez, csb, is the first bishop of Las Cruces, New Mexico. Presently he is also chair of the U.S. Bishops' Subcommittee on Hispanic Liturgy.

Reverend Arturo Pérez Rodríguez is a priest of the Archdiocese of Chicago who lectures and writes on liturgy and spirituality within the Hispanic community. He is currently administrator of Assumption Parish and acting director of Kolbe House, the Archdiocese of Chicago's parish-based ministry for those in jail and their families.

Reverend David G. Sánchez is the administrator of St. Joseph Catholic Church and the coordinator of Hispanic Latino Communities in Region VII of the Archdiocese of Louisville in Kentucky.

Juan J. Sosa was ordained in 1972. Father Sosa is pastor of St. Catherine of Siena Catholic Church in Miami and adjunct professor at both Florida seminaries. Previously the executive director of the Ministry of Worship and Spiritual Life in the Archdiocese of Miami, Father Sosa is currently the chair of the Committee on Popular Piety. An advisor to the U.S. Bishops' Committee on the Liturgy, Father Sosa has twice been president of the Instituto Nacional Hispano de Liturgia.

Luis A. Vera, OSA, D. Min., was born and raised in Puerto Rico. Prior and director of pre-novices at Augustinian College in Washington, D.C., he sits on the advisory board of the Instituto Nacional Hispano de Liturgia and the board of the Academy of Catholic Hispanic Theologians of the United States. He is also retreat director and a member of the board of trustees of Villanova University, Villanova, Pennsylvania.

Sister Dominga Maria Zapata, SH, is a native of Puerto Rico and member of the religious community of the Society of Helpers. She was a member of the coordinating teams of all the National Hispanic Pastoral Encuentros. Sister Dominga has also been part of the Paulist National Catholic Evangelization Association as a member of its Evangelizing Mission Teams for over five years. She coordinates the development of a house of Hispanic spirituality under the name of El Pozo del Peregrino in Chicago. She is an *acompañante espiritual* (spiritual director) and teaches in various Hispanic formation programs.

Joyce Ann Zimmerman, C.PP.S., is a Precious Blood sister and the director of the Institute for Liturgical Ministry in Dayton, Ohio; an adjunct professor of liturgy; founding editor of *Liturgical Ministry*; award-winning author; and frequent speaker at liturgical conferences and workshops.

BIBLIOGRAPHY

Articles

Arias, Miguel. 2007. "Stay with Me." *U.S. Catholic* 72(4): 48.

Awalt, Barbe, and Paul Rhetts. 1998. "The Images of *Nuestra Señora* in New Mexican Devotional Art: Traditional and Contemporary." *Marian Studies* 49: 19–40.

Bannon, Anne Louise. 2001. "Hispanic/Latino Faith Strong, Diverse." CARA Report 6(4): 4.

Beatty, Andrew. 2006. "The Pope in Mexico: Syncretism in Public Ritual." *American Anthropologist* 108(2): 324–335.

Bonnot, Bernard R., Thomas Boomershine, and Brian Sweeney. 2001. "A Liturgical Via Media." *America* 185 (November 5): 14.

Brancatelli, Robert J. 2003. "*Religiosidad Popular* as a Form of Liturgical Catechesis." *Worship* 77(3): 210–224.

Burgaleta, Claudio. 2006. "Preaching the Teaching: Hispanics, Homiletics, and Catholic Social Justice Doctrine." *Theological Studies* 67(3): 702–703.

Cahn, Peter. 2005. "Saints with Glasses: Mexican Catholics in Alcoholics Anonymous." *Journal of Contemporary Religion* 20(2): 217–229.

Campo-Flores, Arian. 2005. "The Battle for Latino Souls." *Newsweek* 145 (March 21): 50–51.

Casarella, Peter. 1998. "The Painted Word." *Journal of Hispanic/ Latino Theology* 4(2): 18–42.

Cassese, Giacomo. 2000. "De la Iglesia y el Estado Omnipotente: ¿Cómo Debemos Vivir la Fe en el Imperio?" *Apuntes* 20(3): 104–117.

Cavazos-González, Gilberto. 2002. "Whom Will You Welcome This Christmas?" *U.S. Catholic* 67(12): 12–15.

Colle, Marie-Pierre. 2005. "Portraits of Our Lady." *U.S. Catholic* 70(12): 34–38.

Colonna, Dominic. 2002. "Theology of New Mexican Folk Art: The Arroyo Seco Trinity." *Listening* 37(3): 172–183.

Corona, Ignacio. 1997. "Guadalupanism: Popular Religion and Cultural Identity." *Josephinum Journal of Theology* 4 (Supplement): 6–22.

Craven, Scott. 2001. "A Marriage of Aztec, Catholic Cultures." *Hispanic Times Magazine* 24(4): 16.

Csordas, Thomas J., and Elizabeth Lewton. 1998. "Practice, Performance, and Experience in Ritual Healing." *Transcultural Psychiatry* 35(4): 435–512.

Daly, Les. 1999. "Get Muddy, Save a Church: Regular Mudding Events Keep Church and Tradition Intact for the Hispanic Communities of Northern New Mexico." *Smithsonian* (December): 122+.

Davalos, Karen Mary. 2004. "The Via Crucis in Chicago: A Reflection on/of Grace." *American Catholic* 115(2): 97–100.

Davis, Kenneth G. 1997. "A New Catholic Reformation?" *Chicago Studies* 36(3): 216–223.

———. 1999. "When a Bilingual Preacher Is Made, Not Born." *AIM* (Winter): 18–20.

———. 2000. "Cross-Cultural Preaching." *Chicago Studies* 39 (Autumn–Winter): 233–253.

———. 2002. "Naturalismo." *AAR Abstracts* (November): 123.

———. 2003. "Preacher, Exegete Thyself: To Those Who Preach in Spanish as a Second Language." *Church* 19(3): 25–26.

———. 2004. "Annoying the Sick?: Cultural Considerations for the Celebration of a Sacrament." *Worship* 78(1): 35–50.

———. 2005a. "Hispanic Popular Catholicism." *Pastoral Life* 54(3) March: 35–50.

———. 2005b. "The Baptismal Garment Is Seamless: A Hispanic Model for Whole-Community Celebration." *Ministry and Liturgy* 32(10): 14–17.

———. 2006a. "Concentrate Consecrate: Hispanic Home Rituals and the Liturgy of the Catholic Church." *Liturgy* 21(4): 53–60.

———. 2006b. "Dead Reckoning or Reckoning with the Dead: Hispanic Catholic Funeral Customs." *Liturgy* 21(1): 21–27.

———. 2006c. "Guadalupe: Mary Clothed with the Sun." *Emmanuel* 112(6): 528–530.

———. 2006d. "One Faith, Many Cultures." *St. Anthony Messenger* (June): 25–28.

———. 2006e. "Quintessential *Quinceañera* Questions." *Today's Liturgy* Ordinary Time I (June 11–September 2): 20–24.

Davis, Kenneth G., and Carmen María Cervantes. 1997. "La Catequesis ante la Experiencia Religiosa." *Catequética* 1 (Enero/Marzo): 3–8.

Davis, Kenneth G., and David Sánchez. 2003. "Preaching in Spanish." *Ministry and Liturgy*. 30(4): 12–14.

Del Valle, David. 1998. "A Caveat for *El Barrio*." Apuntes 18 (Summer): 51–55.

Díaz-Stevens, Ana María. 1998. "Syncretism, Popular Religiosity, and Communitarian Spirituality among Puerto Ricans and Hispanics in the United States." *Listening* 33(3): 162–174.

———. 1999. "Memory, Imagination, and Tradition: Diasporic Latino Spirituality." *Union Seminary Quarterly Review* 53(1–2): 1–18.

Empereur, James L. 1998. "Popular Religion and the Liturgy: The State of the Question." *Liturgical Ministry* 7 (Summer): 105–120.

———. 2005. "Anointing: Ancient Sacrament, New Issues." *Ministry & Liturgy* 32(3): 10–11.

Espín, Orlando O. 2006. "Whose Lex Orandi? Whose Lex Credendi? Latino/a Catholicism as a Theological Challenge for Liturgy." *Proceedings of the North American Academy of Liturgy* January 5–8: 53–71.

Faiola, Anthony. 2007. "In U.S., Hispanics Bring Catholicism to Its Feet: The Church Offers Livelier Services for a Growing Constituency of Charismatics." *The Washington Post*, May 7, p. A01.

Fernández, Santiago. 2004. "*Tres Reyes Magos*, Many Cultures." *Pastoral Music* 28(4): 27–29.

Francis, Mark. 1998a. "The Challenge of Worship in a Multi-Cultural Assembly." *Liturgy* 14(4): 3–9.

———. 1998b. "The Hispanic Liturgical Year: The People's Calendar." *Liturgical Ministry* 7 (Summer): 129–135.

Galles, Duane. 1997. "The Hispanic Musical Presence in the New Evangelization in the United States!" *Sacred Music* 124(2): 6–11.

García, Mario T. 2000. "The Chicano Southwest: Catholicism and Its Meaning." *U.S. Catholic Historian* 18(4): 1–24.

García, Sixto J. 1999. "Hispanic Theologians as Actors, Poets and Prophets of Their Communities." *Journal of Hispanic/Latino Theology* 6 (May): 5–18.

García-Rivera, Alejandro. 1997. "A Matter of Presence." *Journal of Hispanic/Latino Theology* 5(2): 22–53.

Gilhooley, James. 2005. "Mexican Saint Bears Witness to the Poor: Devotion to St. José María Spreads to America." *Our Sunday Visitor* 93(45): 9.

Goizueta, Roberto S. 1997. "San Fernando Cathedral: Incarnating the Theology Born of the Mexican American Cultural Center." *Listening* 32(3): 190–202.

———. 2004. "The Symbolic Realism of U.S. Latino/a Popular Catholicism." *Theological Studies* 65(2): 255–274.

Gómez, Raúl. 1997. "The Day of the Dead: Celebrating the Continuity of Life and Death." *Liturgy* 14(1): 28–40.

———. 2000. "Preaching the Ritual Masses among Latinos." *Chicago Studies* 39 (Autumn–Winter): 295–311.

———. 2005. "Preaching and the Quinceañera." *Preach* (March/April): 11–12.

González, Justo. 1997. "Reading Ourselves in Spanish." *Apuntes* 17(1): 12–17.

Groody, Daniel G. 2006. "Fruit of the Vine and Work of Human Hands: Immigration and the Eucharist." *Worship* 80(5): 386–403.

Gutiérrez, Lisa. 2006. "Sumptuous Sweet 15: As Hispanics' Quinceañeras Get More Popular, Many Get More Lavish." *Kansas City Star*, June 7.

Hoffman, Richard. 2005–6. "A Wave of Spirituality." *Hispanic* 18(12): 44–45.

Irvine, Andrew. 2000. "Mestizaje and the Problem of Authority." *Journal of Hispanic/Latino Theology* 8(1): 5–37.

Jiménez, Pablo. 1997a. "From Text to Sermon." *Apuntes* 17(2): 35–40.

———. 1997b. "The Laborers of the Vineyard (Matthew 20:1–16): A Hispanic Homiletical Reading." *Journal for Preachers* 21(1): 35–40.

Johnson, Maxwell. 2004. "The Feast of the Virgin of Guadalupe and the Season of Advent." *Worship* 78(6): 482–499.

Kolar, Peter M. 1998. "Useful Tips for Gringos Ministering with Hispanics." *Liturgy* 90(29): 4–7.

Lasalle Klein, Robert. 1998. "The Body of Christ: The Claim of the Crucified People on U.S. Theology and Ethics." *Journal of Hispanic/Latino Theology* 5 (May): 48–77.

Lefebure, Leo D. 2000. "Preaching and Culture: Engaging U.S. Hispanic Congregations." *Chicago Studies* 39 (Autumn–Winter): 229–331.

Lobra, Sandra, JoAnn Youngblut, and Dorothy Brooten. 2006. "Cross-Cultural Beliefs, Ceremonies, and Rituals Surrounding Death of a Loved One." *Pediatric Nursing* 32(1): 44–50.

Machado, Daisy L. 1997. "From Anglo-American Traditions to a Multicultural World." *Discipliana* 57 (Summer): 47–60.

Manalo, Ricky. 2006. "Ethnic Celebrations." *Rite* 37(5): 15.

Martell-Otero, Loida I. 2001. "Of *Satos* and Saints: Salvation from the Periphery." *Perspectivas: Occasional Papers* 4 (Summer): 7–35.

Martin, James. 2003. "Contemporary Catholics on Traditional Devotions." *America* 188 (March 31): 18.

Martínez, Diego. 2004. "*Las Posadas*: Processing with Los Peregrinatos Santos." *Pastoral Music* 28(4): 24–26.

Matovina, Timothy M. 1997. "New Frontiers of Guadalupanismo." *Journal of Hispanic/Latino Theology* 5(1): 20–36.

———. 1998a. "Hispanic Faith and Theology." *Theology Today* 54(4): 507–511.

———. 1998b. "San Fernando Cathedral and the Alamo: Sacred Place, Public Ritual, and Construction of Meaning." *Journal of Ritual Studies* 12(2): 1–13.

———. 2003. "Our Lady of Guadalupe: Patroness of América." *America* 189 (December 8): 8–12.

Maynard-Reid, Pedrito U. 2003. "Diverse Worship: African-American, Caribbean and Hispanic Perspectives." *Apuntes* 23(4): 156–158.

Mejido, Manuel J. 1999. "Theoretical Prolegomenon to the Sociology of U.S. Hispanic Popular Religion." *Journal of Hispanic/Latino Theology* 7 (August): 27–55.

———. 2002. "Propaedeutic to the Critique of the Study of U.S. Hispanic Religion: A Polemic Against Intellectual Assimilation." *Journal of Hispanic/Latino Theology* 10(2): 31–63.

Miranda, Carolina. 2004. "Fifteen Candles." *Time* 164 (July 19): 83.

Myers, Kathleen Ann. "Spanish American Saints and the Rhetoric of Identity, 1600–1810." *Catholic Historic Review* 89(3): 570–572.

Novoa, Ana. 2004/2005. "Lessons from La Morenita del Tepeyac." *Journal of Law & Religion* 20(1): 267–294.

Odem, Mary. 2004. "Our Lady of Guadalupe in the New South: Latino Immigrants and the Politics of Integration in the Catholic Church." *Journal of American Ethnic History* 24(1): 26–57.

Pérez Rodríguez, Arturo. 1997. "Mestizo Liturgy: A Mestizaje of the Roman and Hispanic Rites of Worship." *Liturgical Ministry* 6 (Summer): 141–147.

Pérez y Mena, Andrés I. 1998. "Cuban Santería, Haitian Vodun, Puerto Rican Spiritualism: A Multi-culturalist Inquiry into Syncretism." *Journal for the Scientific Study of Religion* 37(1): 15–27.

Pineda, Ana María. 2000. "The Murals: Rostros del Pueblo." *Journal of Hispanic/Latino Theology* 8(2): 5–17.

———. 2004. "*Imágenes de Dios en el Camino: Retablos*, Ex-votos, *Milagritos*, and Murals." *Theological Studies* 65(2): 364–379.

Poyo, Gerald E. 2002. " 'Integration Without Assimilation': Cuban Catholics in Miami, 1960–1980." *U.S. Catholic Historian* 20 (Fall): 91–109.

Pulido, Alberto Lopéz. 2000. "Sacred Expressions of the Popular: An Examination of *Los Hermanos Penitentes* of New Mexico and *Los Hermanos Cheos* of Puerto Rico." *Centro Journal* 11(2): 56–69.

Reza, Mary Frances. 2004. "Devotion to *Los Santos*." *Pastoral Music* 28(4): 35–38.

Riebe-Estrella, Gary. 1998. "Latino Religiosity or Latino Catholicism?" *Theology Today* 54(4): 512–515.

———. 1999. "*La Virgen*: A Mexican Perspective." *New Theology Review* 12(2): 39–47.

Rieff, David. 2006. "Nuevo Catholics." *New York Times*, December 24, Section 6, p. 40–87.

Rodríguez, Jeanette. 1997. "Contemporary Encounters with Guadalupe." *Journal of Hispanic/Latino Theology* 5(1): 48–60.

———. 2004. "Mestiza Spirituality: Community, Ritual, and Justice." *Theological Studies* 65(2): 317–339.

Rogers, Thomas, and Mauro B. de Souza. 2003. "Preaching Cross-Culturally to Spanish-Speaking U.S. Hispanic Americans." *Homiletic* 28(1): 1–10.

Royal, Robert. 2004. "Hispanic Peril—or Promise? [Seeing Things]." *Crisis* (May): 44–45.

Rubio, José Antonio. 1998. "Checklist for Multicultural and Multilingual Worship." *Liturgy* 14(4): 23–26.

Sell, Barry. "The Origins of Mexican Catholicism: Nahua Rituals and Sacraments in Sixteenth-Century Mexico." *Hispanic American Historical Review* 86(1): 145–146.

Siems, Larry. 1999. "Loretta Sánchez and the Virgin." *Aztlán* 24(1): 153–173.

Sikkink, David, and Edwin I. Hernández. 2004. "Family Religiosity Important to Latino School Success." *CARA Report* 9(3): 11.

Sosa, Juan J. 1998. "Textos Litúrgicos para los Católicos Hispanos en los Estados Unidos." *Liturgia y Canción* 9(3): 12–21.

———. 1999. "Liturgy and Popular Piety: A Marriage Made on Earth." *Church* 15(3): 13–16.

———. 2000. "Preaching and Popular Religion." *Chicago Studies* 39 (Autumn–Winter): 285–294.

———. 2004. "Viernes Santo: A Pilgrimage with Christ on the Cross." *Pastoral Music* 28(4): 32–34.

Stevens-Arroyo, Antonio M. 2004. "Characteristics of Latino Lay Ministers." *CARA Report* 9(4): 9.

Thompson, John. 1998. "*Santísima Muerte:* On the Origin and Development of a Mexican Occult Image." *Journal of the Southwest* 40(4): 405–436.

Tirres, Chris. 2007. "Guadalupe and Her Faithful: Latino Catholics in San Antonio, from Colonial Origins to the Present." *Journal of the American Academy of Religion* 75(1): 227–230.

Torres, Theresa. 2006. "Homilies with an Eye on Hispanic Life." *National Catholic Reporter* 42 (January 20): 10a.

Vera, Alexandrina D. 1998. "Guitars in Hispanic Liturgy Today." *Pastoral Music* 22 (January): 32–35.

Vera, Louis. 2004. "The Kiss of Peace: An Hispanic Understanding." *New Theology Review* 17(4): 30–39.

Viladrich, Anahí. 2006. "Beyond the Supernatural: Latino Healers Treating Latino Immigrants in NYC." *Journal of Latino/Latin American Studies* 2(1): 134–148.

Wakin, Daniel. 2003. "Latino Church Greets Its New Home With a Procession of the Faithful." *New York Times*, April 14, p. F1.

Wilcox, W. Bradford. 2002. "Then Comes Marriage?: Religion, Race, and Marriage in Urban America." *CRRUCS Report* 2002.

Wright, Robert E. 1998. "Popular Religiosity: Review in Literature." *Liturgical Ministry* 7 (Summer): 141–146.

Zimmerman, Joyce Ann, ed. 1997. "Inculturation." *Liturgical Ministry* 6 (Summer): 97–150.

Chapters in Edited Books

Davis, Kenneth G. 1999. "*Sensus Fidelium*: Vehículo para la Inculturación en Culturas Concretas." Pp. 120–127 in *Abrir Caminos a la Vida*. Edited by Rosemarie Kamke. Rome: Institución Teresiana.

———. 2006. "Health and Healing." In *Handbook of Latina/o Theologies*. Edited by Edwin Aponte and Miguel A. De La Torre. St. Louis, MO: Chalice Press.

De Luna, Anita. 2006. "Popular Religion and Spirituality." In *Handbook of Latina/o Theologies*. Edited by Edwin Aponte and Miguel A. De La Torre. St. Louis, MO: Chalice Press.

Durand, Jorge. 1998. "Migration and Integration: Intermarriages among Mexicans and Non-Mexicans in the United States." Pp. 209–221 in *Crossings: Mexican Immigration in Interdisciplinary Perspective*. Edited by Marcelo M. Suárez-Orozco. Cambridge, MA: Harvard University Press.

Empereur, James L. 1999. "The Cultural Bodies of Worship." Pp. 85–104 in *Bodies of Worship: Explorations in Theory and Practice*. Edited by Bruce T. Morrill. Collegeville, MN: Liturgical Press.

Espín, Orlando O. 2006. "Traditioning: Culture, Daily Life and Popular Religion, and Their Impact on Christian Tradition." Pp. 1–22 in *Futuring Our Past: Explorations in the Theology of Tradition*. Edited by Orlando O. Espín and Gary Macy. Maryknoll, NY: Orbis Books.

Falicov, Celia J. 1999. "Religion and Spiritual Folk Traditions in Immigrant Families: Therapeutic Resources with Latinos." Pp. 104–120 in *Spiritual Resources in Family Therapy*. Edited by Froma Walsh. New York: Guilford Press.

Fernández, Eduardo C. 2006. "Sacraments." In *Handbook of Latina/o Theologies*. Edited by Edwin Aponte and Miguel A. De La Torre. St. Louis, MO: Chalice Press.

Figueroa Deck, Allan. 1999. "Latino Popular Religion and the Struggle for Justice." Pp. 139–210 in *Religion, Race, and Justice in a Changing America.* Edited by Gary Orfield and Holly Lebowitz Rossi. New York: A Century Foundation Book.

———. 2004. "Evangelization as Conceptual Framework for the Church's Mission: The Case of U.S. Hispanics." Pp. 85–110 in *Evangelizing America.* Edited by Thomas P. Rausch. New York: Paulist Press.

García-Treto, Francisco O. 2003. "The Word Off Center: Preaching at the Margins." Pp. 142–152 in *Just Preaching.* Edited by André Resner. St. Louis, MO: Chalice Press.

Goizueta, Roberto S. 1999. "Fiesta: Life in the Subjunctive." Pp. 84–99 in *From the Heart of Our People: Latino/a Explorations in Catholic Systematic Theology.* Edited by Orlando O. Espín and Miguel H. Díaz. Maryknoll, NY: Orbis Books.

———. 2006. "Making Christ Credible: U.S. Latino/a Popular Catholicism and the Liberating Nearness of God." Pp. 169–178, 302 in *Practicing Catholic: Ritual, Body, and Contestation in Catholic Faith.* Edited by Bruce Morrill, Joanna Ziegler, and Susan Rodgers. New York: Palgrave Macmillan.

González, Justo L. 1998. "A Hispanic Perspective: By the Rivers of Babylon." Pp. 80–97, 162–163 in *Preaching Justice: Ethnic and Cultural Perspectives.* Edited by Christine M. Smith. Cleveland, OH: United Church Press.

Hernández-Ávila, Inés. 2005. "La Mesa del Santo Niño de Atocha and the Conchero Dance Tradition of Mexico-Tenochtitlán: Religious Healing in Urban Mexico and the United States." Pp. 359–374 in *Religion and Healing in America.* Edited by Linda Barnes and Susan Starr Sered. New York: Oxford University Press.

Jensen, Carol L. 1997. "Roman Catholicism in Modern New Mexico: A Commitment to Survive." Pp. 1–26 in *Religion in Modern New Mexico.* Edited by Ferenc M. Szasz and Richard W. Etulain. Albuquerque, NM: University of New Mexico Press.

Jiménez, Pablo A. 2005. "Toward a Postcolonial Homiletic: Justo L. Gonzalez's Contribution to Hispanic Preaching." Pp. 159–167 in *Hispanic Christian Thought at the Dawn of the 21st Century: Apuntes in Honor of Justo L. Gonzalez.* Edited by Alvin Padilla, Roberto Goizueta, and Eldin Villfane. Nashville, TN: Abingdon Press.

Juárez, José Roberto. 2001. "Hispanics, Catholicism, and the Legal Academy." Pp. 163–75 in *Christian Perspectives on Legal Thought.* Edited by Michael W. McConnell, Robert F. Cochran Jr., and Angela C. Carmella. New Haven, CT: Yale University Press.

Martínez, Marcos. 1998. "Community and the Sacred in Chicano Theater." Pp. 312–324 in *El Cuerpo de Cristo: The Hispanic Experience in the U.S. Catholic Church.* Edited by Peter J. Casarella and Raúl Gómez. New York: Crossroad.

McGuire, Brian and Duncan Scrymgeour. 1998. "*Santería* and *Curanderismo* in Los Angeles." Pp. 211–222 in *New Trends and Developments in African Religions.* Edited by Peter B. Clarke. Westport, CT: Greenwood Press.

Medina, Lara. 2005. "Communing with the Dead: Spiritual and Cultural Healing in Chicano/a Communities." Pp. 205–215 in *Religion and Healing in America.* Edited by Linda Barnes and Susan Starr Sered. New York: Oxford University Press.

Nickoloff, James. 2006. "The Paradoxical Character of Symbols, Popular Religion, and Church: Questions for U.S. Latino/a Theology." Pp. 179–182, 303 in *Practicing Catholic: Ritual, Body, and Contestation in Catholic Faith.* Edited by Bruce Morrill, Joanna Ziegler, and Susan Rodgers. New York: Palgrave Macmillan.

Pineda, Ana María. 1997. "Hospitality." Pp. 29–42 in *Practicing Our Faith: A Way of Life for a Searching People.* Edited by Dorothy C. Bass. San Francisco: Jossey-Bass.

Polk, Patrick A., et al. 2005. "Miraculous Migrants to the City of Angels: Perceptions of El Santo Niño de Atocha and San Simón as Sources of Health and Healing." Pp. 103–120 in *Religion and Healing in America.* Edited by Linda Barnes and Susan Starr Sered. New York: Oxford University Press.

Recinos, Harold J. 2001. "Popular Religion, Political Identity, and Life-Story Testimony in an Hispanic Community." Pp. 116–128 in *Ties That Bind: The African-American and Hispanic-American/Latino(a) Theologies in Dialogue*. Edited by Anthony B. Pinn and Benjamin Valentin. London: Continuum.

Ruíz Baia, Larissa. 2001. "Rethinking Transnationalism: National Identities among Peruvian Catholics in New Jersey." Pp. 147–164 in *Christianity, Social Change, and Globalization in the Americas*. Edited by Anna L. Peterson, Manuel A. Vásquez, and Philip J. Williams. Brunswick, NJ: Rutgers University Press.

Rushing, J. Rhett. "Homemade Religion: Miraculous Images of Jesus and the Virgin Mary in South Texas." Pp. 267–275 in *2001: A Texas Folklore Odyssey*. Edited by Francis Edward Abernethy. Denton, TX: University of North Texas Press.

Sauceda-Chavez, Teresa. 2006. "Sacred Space/Public Identity." In *Handbook of Latina/o Theologies*. Edited by Edwin Aponte and Miguel A. De La Torre. St. Louis, MO: Chalice Press.

Sullivan, Kathleen. 2000. "St. Mary's Catholic Church: Celebrating Domestic Religion." Pp. 125–140 in *Religion and the New Immigrants: Continuities and Adaptations in Immigrant Congregations*. Edited by Helen Ebaugh and Janet Saltzman Chafetz. Walnut Creek, CA: AltaMira Press.

Vásquez, Manuel A. 2001a. "Battling Spiritism and the Need for Catholic Orthodoxy." Pp. 449–461 in *Religions of the United States in Practice*. Edited by Colleen McDannell. Vol. II. Princeton, NJ: Princeton University Press.

———. 2001b. "Charismatic Renewal among Latino Catholics." Pp. 346–354 in *Religions of the United States in Practice*. Edited by Colleen McDannell. Vol. II. Princeton, NJ: Princeton University Press.

Books

Abernethy, Francis Edward. 2001. *2001: A Texas Folklore Odyssey*. Denton, TX: University of North Texas Press.

Aponte, Edwin D., and Miguel De La Torre, eds. 2006. *Handbook of Latina/o Theologies*. St. Louis, MO: Chalice Press.

Arias, Miguel, Mark Francis, and Arturo Pérez-Rodríguez. 2000. *La Navidad Hispana at Home and at Church*. Chicago: Liturgy Training Publications.

Awalt, Barbe, and Paul Rhetts. 1997. *Our Saints Among Us: 400 Years of New Mexican Devotional Art*. Albuquerque, NM: LPD Press.

Barnes, Linda, and Susan Starr Sered, eds. 2005. *Religion and Healing in America*. New York: Oxford University Press.

Bass, Dorothy C., ed. 1997. *Practicing Our Faith: A Way of Life for a Searching People*. San Francisco: Jossey-Bass.

Brading, David. 2003. *Mexican Phoenix: Our Lady of Guadalupe: Image and Tradition across Five Centuries*. New York: Cambridge University Press.

Casarella, Peter J., and Raúl Gómez, eds. 1998. *El Cuerpo de Cristo: the Hispanic Presence in the U.S. Catholic Church*. New York: Crossroad.

Chávez, Eduardo. 2006. *Our Lady of Guadalupe and Saint Juan Diego: The Historical Evidence*. Lanham, MD: Rowman & Littlefield Publishers.

Chávez Candelaria, Cordelia, Arturo J. Aldama, Peter J. García, eds. 2004. *Encyclopedia of Latino Popular Culture*. Westport, CT: Greenwood Press.

Clarke, Peter B., ed. 1998. *New Trends and Developments in African Religions*. Westport, CT: Greenwood Press.

Cunningham, Lawrence. 2001. *Popular Devotions*. London: Way Publications.

Dahm, Charles P. 2004. *Pastoral Ministry in a Hispanic Community*. New York: Paulist Press.

Davis, Kenneth G., ed. 1997. *Misa, Mesa y Musa: Liturgy in the U.S. Hispanic Church*. Schiller Park, IL: World Library Publications.

Davis, Kenneth G. 2002. *El Recacer de los Jóvens/The Renewal of Youth*. Staten Island, NY: Alba House.

Davis, Kenneth G., Eduardo C. Fernández, and Verónica Méndez, eds. 2002. *United States Hispanic Catholics: Trends and Works, 1990–2000*. Scranton, PA: Scranton University Press.

Davis, Kenneth G., and Leopoldo Peréz, eds. 2004. *Preaching the Teaching: Hispanics, Homiletics, and Catholic Social Justice Doctrine*. Scranton, PA: University of Scranton Press.

Davis, Kenneth G., and Jorge L. Presmanes, eds. 2000. *Preaching and Culture in Latino Congregations.* Chicago: Liturgy Training Publications.

De La Torre, Miguel, and Edwin Aponte, eds. 2001. *Introducing Latino/a Theologies.* Maryknoll, NY: Orbis Books.

De Luna, Anita. 2002. *Faith Formation and Popular Religion: Lessons from the Tejano Experience.* Lanham, MD: Rowman & Littlefield Publishers.

Díaz-Stevens, Ana María, and Anthony M. Stevens-Arroyo. 1998. *Recognizing the Latino Resurgence in U.S. Religion: The Emmaus Paradigm.* Boulder, CO: Westview Press.

Dolan, Jay, and Allan Figueroa Deck, eds. 1997. *Hispanic Catholic Culture in the U.S.: Issues and Concerns.* Notre Dame, IN: University of Notre Dame Press.

Ebaugh, Helen, and Janet Saltzman Chafetz, eds. 2000. *Religion and the New Immigrants: Continuities and Adaptations in Immigrant Congregations.* Walnut Creek, CA: AltaMira Press.

————. 2002. *Religion Across Borders: Transnational Immigrant Networks.* New York: AltaMira Press.

Elizondo, Virgilio P. 1997. *Guadalupe: Mother of the New Creation.* Maryknoll, NY: Orbis Books.

Elizondo, Virgilio P., and Timothy M. Matovina. 1998a. *Mestizo Worship: A Pastoral Approach to Liturgical Ministry.* Collegeville, MN: Liturgical Press.

————. 1998b. *San Fernando Cathedral: Soul of the City.* Maryknoll, NY: Orbis Books.

Empereur, James, and Eduardo Fernández. 2006. *La Vida Sacra: Contemporary Hispanic Sacramental Theology.* Lanham, MD: Rowman & Littlefield Publishers.

Erevia, Angela. 2000. *Quince Años: Celebrando La Vida—Celebrating Life.* San Antonio, TX: Missionary Catechists of Divine Providence.

Espín, Orlando O. 1997. *The Faith of the People.* Maryknoll, NY: Orbis Books.

Espín, Orlando O., and Miguel H. Díaz. 1999. *From the Heart of Our People: Latino/a Explorations in Catholic Systematic Theology.* Maryknoll, NY: Orbis Books.

Espín, Orlando O., and Gary Macy, eds. 2006. *Futuring Our Past: Explorations in the Theology of Tradition*. Maryknoll, NY: Orbis Books.

Fisher-San Juan, Richard D. 1997. *The Virgin of Guadalupe: Artistic Expressions of Love and Beauty on the U.S.-Mexico Frontier*. Tucson, AZ: Sunracer Publications.

Gómez, Raúl, ed. *Languages of Worship/El Lenguaje de la Liturgia*. 2004. Chicago: Liturgy Training Publications.

Gómez, Raúl, and Heliodoro Lucatero. 1997. *Don y Promesa: Costumbres y Tradiciones en los Ritos Matrimoniales Hispanos*. Portland, OR: Oregon Catholic Press.

Gómez-Ruíz, Raúl. 2007. *Mozarabs, Hispanics, and the Cross*. Maryknoll, NY: Orbis Books.

Gonzáles, Justo L., and Pablo Jiménez, eds. 2005. *Púlpito: An Introduction to Hispanic Preaching*. Nashville: Abingdon Press.

Griffith, James S. 2003. *Folk Saints of the Borderlands: Victims, Bandits & Healers*. Tucson, AZ: Rio Nuevo Publishers.

Gutiérrez, José Roberto, director. 1999. *Un Pueblo Sacramental/A Sacramental People*. Chicago: Liturgy Training Publications. 90 minutes. 3 Videocassettes.

Hoyt-Goldsmith, Diane. 2002. *Celebrating a Quinceañera: A Latina's 15th Birthday Celebration*. New York: Holiday House.

Johnson, Lawrence, Rosa María Icaza, and Miguel Arias. 2005. *El Misterio de Fe: Un Estudio de los Elementos Estructurales de la Misa*. 4th ed. Washington, DC: Federation of Diocesan Liturgical Commissions.

Kamke, Rosemarie, ed. 1999. *Abrir Caminos a la Vida*. Rome: Institución Teresiana.

Kanellos, Nicolas. 2004. *Noche Buena: Hispanic American Christmas Stories*. New York: Oxford University Press.

Kolar, Peter M, ed. 1998. *Cantos del Pueblo de Dios*. Franklin Park, IL: World Library Publications.

Lamadrid, Enrique R. 1999. *Pilgrimage to Chimayo: Contemporary Portrait of a Living Tradition* Santa Fe, NM: Museum of New Mexico Press.

Lara, Jaime. 2004. *City, Temple, Stage: Eschatological Architecture and Liturgical Theatrics in New Spain*. Notre Dame, IN: University of Notre Dame Press.

Lebon, Jean. 1986, 89. *How to Understand the Liturgy*. New York: Crossroad.

Matovina, Timothy M. 2005. *Guadalupe and Her Faithful: Latino Catholics in San Antonio, from Colonial Origins to the Present*. Baltimore, MD: Johns Hopkins University Press.

Matovina, Timothy M., Virgilio Elizondo, and Allan Figueroa Deck, eds. 2006. *The Treasure of Guadalupe*. Lanham, MD: Rowman & Littlefield Publishers.

Matovina, Timothy M., and Gerald Poyo, eds. 2000. *¡Presente!: U.S. Latino Catholics from Colonial Origins to the Present*. Maryknoll, NY: Orbis Books.

Matovina, Timothy M., and Gary Riebe-Estrella, eds. 2002. *Horizons of the Sacred: Mexican Traditions in U.S. Catholicism*. Ithaca, NY: Cornell University Press.

Maynard-Reid, Pedrito U. 2000. *Diverse Worship: African-American, Caribbean and Hispanic Perspectives*. Downers Grove, IL: InterVarsity Press.

McDannell, Collen, ed. 2001. *Religions of the United States in Practice*. Vol. II. Princeton, NJ: Princeton University Press.

Menard, Valerie. 2004. *The Latino Holiday Book: From Cinco de Mayo to Dia de los Muertos—The Celebrations and Traditions of Hispanic-Americans*. New York: Marlowe & Company.

Morgan, Ronald. 2002. *Spanish American Saints and the Rhetoric of Identity, 1600–1810*. Tucson, AZ: The University of Arizona Press.

Morrill, Bruce, ed. 1999. *Bodies of Worship: Explorations in Theory and Practice*. Collegeville, MN: Liturgical Press.

Morrill, Bruce, Joanna Ziegler, and Susan Rodgers, eds. 2006. *Practicing Catholic: Ritual, Body, and Contestation in Catholic Faith*. New York: Palgrave Macmillan.

Murrell, N. Samuel, ed. 2000. *Sacred Texts and Human Experience in Caribbean Cultures and Traditions*. New York: St. Martin's Press.

Nabhan-Warren, Kristy. 2005. *The Virgin of El Barrio: Marian Apparitions, Catholic Evangelizing, and Mexican American Activism*. New York: New York University Press.

Orfield, Gary, and Holly Lebowitz Rossi, eds. 1999. *Religion, Race, and Justice in a Changing America*. New York: A Century Foundation Book.

Orsi, Robert, ed. 1999. *Gods of the City: Religion and the American Urban Landscape*. Bloomington, IN: Indiana University Press.

Orsini Dunnington, Jacqueline. 1999. *Guadalupe: Our Lady of New Mexico*. Santa Fe, NM: Museum of New Mexico Press.

Padilla, Alvin, Roberto Goizueta, and Eldin Villfane, eds. 2005. *Hispanic Christian Thought at the Dawn of 21st Century: Apuntes in Honor of Justo L. Gonzalez*. Nashville, TN: Abingdon Press.

Pardo, Osvaldo. 2006. *The Origins of Mexican Catholicism: Nahua Rituals and Christian Sacraments in Sixteenth-Century Mexico*. Ann Arbor, MI: University of Michigan Press.

Pérez-Rodríguez, Arturo and Mark Francis, eds. 1997a. *Primero Dios: Hispanic Liturgical Resource*. Chicago: Liturgy Training Publications.

———. 1997b. *Los Documentos Litúrgicos: Un Recurso Pastoral*. Chicago: Liturgy Training Publications.

Petra, Alexander. 2003. *Mis 15 Años: Manual de Formación Quinceañeras—My 15th Birthday: Teaching Material for Quinceañera Formation*. Boston: Pauline Books & Media.

Phan, Peter C, ed. 2005. *The Directory on Popular Piety and the Liturgy: Principles and Guidelines—A Commentary*. Collegeville, MN: Liturgical Press.

Pinn, Anthony B., and Benjamin Valentin, eds. 2001. *Ties That Bind: The African-American and Hispanic-American/Latino(a) Theologies in Dialogue*. London: Continuum.

Quintero Rivera, Angel G, ed. 2003. *Virgenes, Magos y Escapularios. Imaginería, Etnicidad y Religiosidad Popular en Puerto Rico*. 2nd ed. San Juan, UPR: Centro de Investigaciones Sociales et al.

Rausch, Thomas P., ed. 2004. *Evangelizing America*. New York. Paulist Press.

Richardson, Miles. 2003. *Being-in-Christ and Putting Death in Its Place: An Anthropologist's Account of Christian Performance in Spanish American and the American South*. Baton Rouge, LA: Louisiana State University Press.

Salcedo, Michele. 1997. *Quinceañera: The Essential Guide to Planning the Perfect Sweet Fifteen Celebration*. New York: Henry Holt and Company.

Santiago, Esmeralda, and Joe Davidow, eds. 1999. *Las Christmas: Favorite Latino Authors Share Their Holiday Memories*. London: Vintage.

Smith, Christine M., ed. 1998. *Preaching Justice: Ethnic and Cultural Perspectives.* Cleveland: United Church Press.

Sosa, Juan J. 1999. *Sectas, Cultos y Sincretismos.* Miami, FL: Ediciones Universal.

Steele, Thomas, ed. 2005. *The Alabados of New Mexico.* Albuquerque, NM: University of New Mexico Press.

Súarez-Orozco, Marcelo M., ed. 1998. *Crossings: Mexican Immigration in Interdisciplinary Perspective.* Cambridge, MA: Harvard University Press.

Szasz, Ferenc M., and Richard W. Etulain, eds. 1997. *Religion in Modern New Mexico.* Albuquerque, NM: University of New Mexico Press.

Torres, Larry. 1999. *Six Nuevomexicano Folk Dramas for Advent Season.* Albuquerque, NM: University of New Mexico Press

Treviño, Roberto. 2006. *The Church in the Barrio: Mexican American Ethno-Catholicism in Houston.* Chapel Hill, NC: University of North Carolina Press.

Tweed, Thomas. 1997. *Our Lady of the Exile: Diasporic Religion at a Cuban Catholic Shrine in Miami.* Oxford: Oxford University Press.

Walsh, Froma, ed. 1999. *Spiritual Resources in Family Therapy.* New York: Guilford Press.

Monographs and Dissertations

Andersson, Daniel. 2001. "The Virgin and the Dead: The Virgin of Guadalupe and the Day of the Dead in the Construction of Mexican Identities." Fil.Dr. dissertation, Goteborgs Universitet, Sweden.

Bales, Susan Ridgely. 2002. "Seeing and Being Seen: An Ethnographic Study of Children's Interpretations of First Communion at Two Southern Churches." Ph.D. dissertation, The University of North Carolina at Chapel Hill.

Berman, Sharon. 2005. "*El Santero Zurdo*: The Left-Handed Painter of Saints." M.A. thesis, University of Southern California.

Bolarte, Ruth. 2006. "An Integrative Spiritual Formation Program for Hispanic/Latino Lay People in the Roman Catholic Church in the United States." D.Min dissertation, The Catholic University of America.

Brancatelli, Robert Jaime. 2001. "*Religiosidad Popular* in Contemporary Magisterial Documents and Hispanic-American Theology (1975–1997): An Analysis and Critique." Ph.D. dissertation, The Catholic University of America.

Christian, Barbara Marie. 2000. "Folk Catholicism in the Works of Six United States Latina Writers." Ph.D. dissertation, Indiana University of Pennsylvania.

Condon, Thomas Michael. 1998. "Guidelines and Strategies for Effective Preaching in Multicultural Settings." D.Min. dissertation, Aquinas Institute of Theology.

Coolidge, Martha. 2005. "*Madre Mestiza:* The Virgin of Guadalupe and the Survival of Nahua Thought in Mexican Catholicism." M.A. thesis, California State University, Dominguez Hills.

Doran, Gerard. 2001. "Family Grief Experience at the Death of a Child in the Mexican American Community." Ph.D. dissertation, Fielding Graduate Institute.

Esqueda-Arteaga, Julia. 2006. "The Relationship between Acculturation, Gender, and Experiences of Grief among Mexican-American Adults." Ph.D. dissertation, Alliant International University, Los Angeles.

Galvéz, Alyshia. 2004. "In the Name of Guadalupe: Religion, Politics and Citizenship Among Mexicans in New York." Ph.D. dissertation, Dept. of Anthropology, New York University.

García, Avelino. 2003. "Christian Baptism: A Program for Lay Leaders in Hispanic Ministry in the Archdiocese of Baltimore, Maryland." D.Min. dissertation, The Catholic University of America.

García, Ricardo. 2001. "Obtaining Consent and Establishing Competence for Marriage Nullity Cases Involving Hispanic Immigrants Who Live in the United States." J.C.L. thesis, The Catholic University of America.

Gravenhorst, Kurt Edward. 2002. "Blessed Art Thou: The Influence of Art on the Rise of the Cult of the Virgin Mary." M.A. thesis, California State University, Dominguez Hills.

Holliday, Karen Veronica. 2003. "Saints as Sinners: Healing and Hegemony in Southern California *Botánicas*." Ph.D. dissertation, University of California, Irvine.

Humberto Díaz, Miguel. 2000. "A Study in United States Hispanic Theological Anthropology, 1972–1999." Ph.D. dissertation, University of Notre Dame.

Lamas, Carmen Esther. 2004. "The Virgen de la Caridad del Cobre and Cuban National Identity." Ph.D. dissertation, University of Pennsylvania.

León, Guillermina. 2005. "The Importance of Music in Hispanic Liturgy: Meeting the Need for Adequate Formation for Music Ministers." M.A. thesis, Catholic Theological Union at Chicago.

Moore, Patricia E. 2000. "*Santos de Santa Fe*: Mediators of Family and Faith, Culture and Place." Ph.D. dissertation, University of New Mexico.

Orozco, Eleazar. 2004. "Narrative Hermeneutics and Homiletics and the Hispanic Culture." D. Min. dissertation, Truett Theological Seminary.

Palacios, Joseph Martin. 2001. "Locating the Social in Social Justice: Social Justice Teaching and Practice in the American and Mexican Catholic Churches." Ph.D. dissertation, Graduate Division, University of California, Berkeley.

Peña, Elaine. 2006. "Making Space Sacred: Devotional Capital, Political Economy, and the Transnational Expansion of the Cult of *la Virgen de Guadalupe*." Ph.D. dissertation, Northwestern University.

Pineda-Madrid, Nancy. 2005. "Interpreting Our Lady of Guadalupe: Mediating the Christian Mystery of Redemption." Ph.D. dissertation, Graduate Theological Union.

Pitti, Gina Marie. 2003. "To 'Hear About God in Spanish': Ethnicity, Church, and Community Activism in the San Francisco Archdiocese's Mexican American Colonias, 1942–1965." Ph.D. dissertation, Department of History, Stanford University.

Quintana Ayala, José L. 2006. "Crafting and Delivering a Local Cross-Cultural Event." D.Min. dissertation, Aquinas School of Theology.

Reed-Bouley, Jennifer. 1998. "Guiding Moral Action: A Study of the United Farm Workers' Use of Catholic Social Teaching and Religious Symbols." Ph.D. dissertation, Loyola University, Chicago.

Stewart, Heather M. 2004. "Señoritas and Princesses: The *Quinceañera* as a Context for Female Development." Ph.D. dissertation, Institute for Clinical Social Work, Chicago.

Sullivan Sandall, Patricia. 2002. "Toward Pastoral and Liturgical Guidelines for the Celebration of the *Quinceañera* at Old Mission Santa Barbara." D.Min. dissertation, Barry University.

Torres, Theresa. 2003. "Our Lady of Guadalupe in the Society of the *Guadalupanas* in Kansas City, Missouri: An Empirical and Theological Analysis." Ph.D. dissertation, The Catholic University of America.

Wainright, Mary. 2002. "Inculturation of the Sunday Liturgy: Welcoming an Emerging Minority Community." Institute in Pastoral Ministries: Integrated Pastoral Research Project.

INDEX